FOREWORD BY JOHN C. MAXWELL

KIRK NOWERY

the STEWARDSHIP *of* LIFE

MAKING THE MOST OF ALL THAT YOU HAVE AND ALL THAT YOU ARE

Published by Spire Resources Inc.
PO Box 180
Camarillo, CA 93011
1-800-992-3060

Cover and text design by Bill Thielker

Printed in the United States of America

ISBN 0-9715828-6-6

TABLE OF CONTENTS

FOREWORD

BY
DR. JOHN C. MAXWELL

I was delighted when Kirk asked me to write the foreword for this book. Kirk Nowery is not only the president of one of my companies (INJOY Stewardship Services), he is also a trusted friend and advisor – one of my "inner circle" members. He adds value to me in so many ways and he is passionate about adding value to pastors and the churches they lead. Because of who Kirk is, I was certain that *The Stewardship of Life* would be compelling on many levels and I was right! This is a book to be read more than once because it is as instructive as it is inspirational (and I can assure you, it *is* inspirational). You will be challenged to think about things of great importance in these seven extraordinary chapters — things that will influence how you look at your time, your commitments, your opportunities and so much more. As the title promises, it addresses Life itself.

Perhaps you have already noticed that the key words of the chapters form an acrostic, VICTORY. Interestingly, this word is not addressed as a main feature of the book. In fact, Kirk never mentions it after the Table of Contents. It is simply there as a subtle reminder that the way to win, the way to experience true personal victory, is through effective stewardship. In order to prepare you for what you're about to discover in this important book, let me say a brief word about each of those seven key factors:

Vision. I have written extensively and spoken frequently on the subject of Vision because it is vital to effective leadership. One cannot be successful in leading or in life without vision, for it enables us to see opportunities and see objectives. However, it is possible to have vision and not use it, to see a goal and not pursue it. This is where the matter of stewardship is crucial: a God-given vision finds its fulfillment through purposeful action. As Kirk explains, many people have big dreams that remain unrealized because they fail to steward the very thing God has put in their hearts. Vision must motivate and encourage you to keep pressing toward the goal. When the goal is clearly seen, life's race is run with greater fervor.

Influence. Several years ago, my friend Jim Dornan and I wrote a book on this subject entitled *Becoming A Person of Influence.* That book emphasizes a priority that Kirk also communicates in this book: Influence must be stewarded wisely and purposefully, and the bedrock of that stewardship is genuine integrity. It was true when your mother first said it to you, and it's true today: honesty is the best policy. She wasn't quoting a Bible verse, but she was stating a biblical truth that we are wise to remember every day. As leaders — and especially as spiritual leaders — we must exemplify true integrity in word and deed. As stewards, this means we must have the character to act with true conviction and to communicate with true information.

Commitment. Without commitment it is difficult (if not impossible) to claim victory in most of life's challenges. Commitment is a determination to keep running even when you're tempted in a moment of weakness or exhaustion to drift off to the side of the track and let other runners pass by. Commitment is also a devotion to what matters, a spiritual fidelity that constantly reminds you of promises to keep and purposes to fulfill. But the inner fire of commitment must be tended, or it can go out. It takes diligent stewardship — stoking the fire and providing the right fuel — to keep commitment burning bright.

Time. The Book of Ecclesiastes teaches us: "There is a time for everything, and a season for every activity under heaven." Understanding time and learning to use it in the most meaningful ways is a vital discipline of the Christian life. Time, like every commodity entrusted to us by God, must be stewarded with wisdom. Of course, in a certain sense, time itself cannot be managed because it goes forward relentlessly; however, what we do within the parameters of time can be managed, and that is what the stewardship of time is all about. As you explore this idea in Chapter 4, I think you will be enlightened and encouraged more than ever to make the most of your time.

Opportunity. We are blessed with so many opportunities in life, and the faithful steward meets them with eagerness and readiness. Building on the foundation of a key Bible passage, Ephesians 5:15-17, Kirk explains how we can "make the most of every opportunity" by stewarding every chance we have to evangelize, empathize and energize — to reach others with the Gospel, to identify with what others think and feel, and to proactively affect how they live. If you are successful in achieving these priorities, you are successful indeed.

Resources. Most Christians, when they hear the word "stewardship" instantly think of money, and there's no getting around that perception. The fact is we shouldn't try to get around that perception because stewardship *does* involve our management of money and our generosity with it. Jesus taught parables on this subject and the apostles wrote about it in the New Testament epistles. All of our monetary and material resources are to be dedicated to the Lord and stewarded for His glory. It is a practical challenge with a spiritual purpose, and it must be handled strategically. I appreciate the way Chapter 6 gives guidance in taking an inventory of resources, following spiritual investment strategies and remembering the insights that really make a difference in the stewardship of resources.

You. I like the title of Chapter 7. "The Stewardship of You" casts a whole new light on a subject that is all too often dull. You may sometimes wonder why, but God has put you in charge of stewarding yourself, of managing your life. He wants to be honored in what you do and how you do it; but He leaves the decisions to you. I was personally challenged by this concluding chapter, especially in what Kirk has written on the call of Moses. It made me realize in a fresh new way how God gives to each of us an extraordinary privilege to steward a precious trust. And, as He asked Moses, the Lord asks each of us, "What is that in *your* hand?"

Legendary football coach Vince Lombardi understood that winning is the result of a process that begins at the most basic level. Holding up the familiar pigskin, he started each year's spring training with the words, "Men, *this* is a football." His purpose was to move from the simple to the complex, concentrating on the essential components which lead to success. That is precisely what this insightful book does in guiding us toward a fuller understanding of biblical stewardship. It covers the basics and then builds on that sure foundation. What we receive in the process is a better grasp of the Stewardship of Life. And, ultimately, what we experience is true Victory.

I believe that you will be blessed and benefited by this book in an unmistakable way. May God give you a heart to receive this important message.

John C. Maxwell
Atlanta, Georgia

Dr. John C. Maxwell is an internationally-renowned speaker and author of numerous *New York Times* bestsellers. He is the Founder of INJOY Stewardship Services, which has partnered with thousands of churches across America to help them raise more than two billion dollars for ministry projects.

THE STEWARDSHIP OF VISION

CHAPTER 1

THE STEWARDSHIP OF VISION

It was without question the most astonishing sight I have ever seen. Even now, many months later, the images are still vibrant in my mind and the feelings are still fresh in my soul.

It happened as monsoon rains fell in Manila, the teeming capital city of the Philippines. I stood on a massive concrete platform that seemed to be floating in a sea of humanity. As far as one could see, there were people. Hundreds of thousands of people. So many people, in fact, that it required photographic evidence to verify the size of that multitude — an amazing 1,000,000 people gathered in one place. On the platform with me were men and women of influence, including the President, Vice President and numerous other national leaders. But on this occasion, they were attending, not leading. Like everyone else, they had come to hear a message of life and hope.

The wind and rain and cool evening air came rushing in like uninvited guests, but nothing could deter the masses of men and women and boys and girls who stood patiently and listened intently. For nearly four hours, as the wind blew relentlessly and the rain continued to fall, they remained alert and attentive. And when the evangelist called upon people to publicly profess their faith in Jesus Christ, they responded. That night, each person who believed in Christ as Savior indicated their decision by filling out a simple yellow card and presenting it to a nearby counselor. The counting of those cards turned out to be a monumental task because over 200,000 were turned in! The follow-up effort, which is still going on, is being conducted by thousands of Filipino churches.

It All Had to Do with Stewardship...

As I relive that unforgettable night in Manila, I am struck by how much it all had to do with stewardship. In fact, virtually every part of that extraordinary experience demanded the wise, strategic stewardship of all that God had entrusted to those who were involved. From the birth of the idea to the shaping of the strategy to the painstaking execution of the plan, stewardship was a constant priority. To me, it was another lesson in the connectedness of the Christian life, reminding me that as believers we are stewards of everything God has given us — vision, influence, commitment, time, opportunity, resources and so much more. All of these are assets to manage for His purposes. They are loaned to us to invest in such a way that we gain the greatest return and He gets the greatest glory.

The journey to that remarkable evening in the Philippines was long and difficult, and it was many years in the making. But even before the first step was taken, there was a vision — a vision of one million people from all ages and all walks of life coming together in one momentous event. The vision was born in the heart of one man, David Janney, my best friend and one of the most gifted leaders I have ever known. Like his namesake in the Bible, David is "a man after God's own heart." With a boldness that is all too rare, he shared the vision with a handful of friends, including myself. "When we go to Manila," he said, "how many people can we expect to preach the Gospel to at one time?" With what we thought was great faith, we replied, "thousands, perhaps tens of thousands." With a wry grin he asked, "Can we believe God for a thousand thousand? Can we look to the future and see one million people gathered together at one time?" And without waiting for a reply, he stated, "I can believe it. I can see it."

Vision, influence, commitment, time, opportunity, resources and so much more. All of these are assets to manage for His purposes. They are loaned to us to invest in such a way that we gain the greatest return and He gets the greatest glory.

David Janney could "see it" because God had given him spiritual vision of a very specific nature. As he described what God had put in his heart, we too were captivated by that same dream and we agreed to trust God to bring it to fruition. We committed our time, our energy and our hearts; and in that moment our small group became stewards of the vision. Admittedly, we had little knowledge of what it would take; but we had boundless expectations for what God was going to do.

The Stewardship of Vision

The stewardship of vision is a vital practice of the Christian life, especially for those who are called to positions of leadership. Like everything else of value to the believer, spiritual vision is a gift of God. It is a divinely empowered ability to see something that doesn't yet exist in the physical realm. When God gives vision, it is something of faith, not of sight; yet it is nonetheless real. Those of us who thought and prayed and prepared for that phenomenal gathering in Manila had countless times envisioned that multitude of one million people. But it wasn't just a big idea that we had conjured up in our minds; it was a concept placed in our hearts by God Himself. And it was by His power and through His provision that the vision was ultimately fulfilled. However, once God had given us that spiritual vision it was up to us to steward it with wisdom, care and due diligence. We had to study all the possible approaches,

> Spiritual vision is a gift of God. It is a divinely empowered ability to see something that doesn't exist in the physical realm. When God gives vision, it is something of faith, not of sight; yet it is nonetheless real.

make complex logistical preparations, conduct numerous preliminary meetings, build a strong coalition, invest a lot of money and spend a lot of time in prayer.

When God calls a man or woman to spiritual leadership in the church, He also gives vision for the fulfillment of that calling. I believe to the core of my being that if God blesses you with an opportunity to lead, He will give you a clear vision of the path and the goal. He will not leave you to fend for yourself, stumbling in darkness and trying to figure out how to move or where to go. He gives vision so that you can move ahead with confidence and certainty.

Ordinary People, Chosen for Extraordinary Moments

Throughout the Bible we see examples of God giving spiritual vision to ordinary people whom He had chosen for extraordinary moments. In the Old Testament era, direct visions from God were a primary means of communicating His will. Several come to mind very readily…

To **Noah**, a man who had never seen rain, God gave the vision of a great flood that would destroy everything on earth.[1]

To **Abraham**, married without children, God gave the vision of a great people of whom he would be the father.[2]

To **Moses,** raised as a prince yet siding with the

slaves, God gave the vision of a great deliverance under his leadership. Though he first ran from the challenge, God would call him back and use him to guide a nation to its place of promise.[3]

Each of these individuals became a steward of a God-given vision. After the revelation came the responsibility — a weighty responsibility to live and think and act in light of what God had revealed.

> Each of these individuals became a steward of a God-given vision. After the revelation came the responsibility — a weighty responsibility to live and think and act in light of what God had revealed.

Noah stewarded the vision by preparing for the calamity to come, warning others as God had warned him. For more than a century — 120 grueling years — he labored to build the vessel that would deliver his family from danger. He was ridiculed, mocked and scorned, but he was not deterred.[4]

Abraham stewarded the vision by setting forth on a journey to a place yet unknown, driven by the hope of a promise yet unfulfilled. Along the way he stumbled often, but he never lost faith in the One whose calling launched his great venture.[5]

Moses, who fled from Egypt and spent 40 lonely years tending sheep in a barren desert, was given a second chance at the ripe young age of 80. From the undying flames of a burning bush, God spoke to Moses and gave him his marching orders. The Lord revealed what was to come, and Moses stewarded the vision by confronting the world's mightiest ruler and demanding his compliance with God's command. Although all the forces of a formidable kingdom were joined against him, Moses led his people in a victorious exodus out of their bondage.[6]

The Artist of Dreams, the Painter of Visions

What an encouragement it is to realize that just as God worked in the lives of His children centuries ago, so He does today. He is still calling ordinary people to follow Him and to experience the abundance of life that only He can give. And He is still the artist of dreams, painting in hearts the vision of what He can and will do.

I am blessed with the opportunity to meet week after week with church leaders across America. In congregations of all shapes and sizes, in communities large and small, I get to hear their stories and listen to their dreams. These are Christians who span the spectrum of denomination, education, temperament, personality, ethnicity and leadership style. The differences between them are profound, yet there are significant things they have in common. They have all answered God's call. They have all sought His guidance. And with spiritual ears they have all heard His voice. To each one, God has given spiritual vision that is uniquely individual. But in every case, the vision is dynamic, not static. It is continually unfolding, taking them "from faith to faith" as they follow their Master's guidance.

One leader who has made an indelible impression upon me is Joel Osteen, senior pastor of Houston's Lakewood Church. Joel is known to millions through Lakewood's far-reaching television program, yet he is not one to wear easily the mantle of celebrity. As the son of a legendary leader, Joel had to find his own way and he knew it would come only in seeking God's one way. After the passing of his father, John Osteen, it fell upon Joel to lead an established congregation into an entirely new era. It was a Joshua-following-Moses type of challenge, and Joel dared to believe God for a bright new vision for the church's future.

> The vision that God etched in Joel's mind was amazingly large: a body of believers numbering not in the thousands but in the tens of thousands. A congregation so sizable that it would take a stadium to hold them.

A Stadium-size Vision

The vision that God etched in Joel's mind was amazingly large: a body of believers numbering not in the thousands but in the tens of thousands — a congregation so sizable that it would take a stadium to hold them. Joel shared the vision with his people and God captivated them with the dream as well. The church began to grow exponentially, and the need for a bigger home became increasingly evident. In the perfection of God's timing, that "home" came on the market. It's known as Compaq Center, and yes, it's a stadium. Formerly home to the Houston Rockets professional basketball team, the Center is ideally situated in the heart of the city, at the second busiest intersection in America. The thought of such a structure being acquired and used by a church was ridiculous to the unbelieving. But through one miraculous occurrence after another, the "ridiculous" became reality.

The company of which I am president, INJOY Stewardship Services, was uniquely blessed to partner with Pastor Osteen, his wife, Victoria, and their exceptional leadership team to raise the capital funds for Lakewood's new home. What a joy it was to see God's people unite in common purpose to give over $52 million to meet the need of such a compelling project. And what a greater joy it will be to see that stadium filled to overflowing with thousands of saints and seekers. And to think: it all began with one man who was willing to steward the vision that God had placed in his heart.

> Vision, in the biblical sense of the word, is spiritual sight. It is always connected to God demonstrating His character and revealing His will.

Spiritual Sight

Vision, in the biblical sense of the word, is spiritual sight. It is always connected to God demonstrating His character and revealing His will. In the Old Testament era especially, God gave visions in order to communicate His purposes. He made Himself known through audible voices, dreams in the night and even a burning bush. God continued to give similar visions into the New Testament era, as we can see from the experiences of Peter, Paul, John and other leaders of the early church. Those men, of course, were used by God to write major portions of Scripture. And when their work was done, just before the end of the first century, the Bible was complete.

God speaks to us today primarily through three means. He gives us instruction and direction through His Word. He converses with us as we converse with Him in prayer. And He guides our thinking and illumines our minds through His Spirit.

Since most Christians never experience a vision like the ones described in the Bible, it's fair to ask why. The simplest answer is that God speaks to us today primarily through three means. He gives us instruction and direction through His Word. He converses with us as we converse with Him in prayer. And He guides our thinking and illumines our minds through His Spirit. As Jesus explained to His disciples, "When he, the Spirit of truth, comes, he will guide you into all truth. He will not speak on his own; he will speak only what he hears, and he will tell you what is yet to come. He will bring glory to me by taking from what is mine and making it known to you."[7] Unlike believers in ancient days, we live in the era of the Spirit; and we have the privilege of His moment-by-moment, day-by-day guidance.

God, who is "the same yesterday, today and forever,"[8] can (and I'm sure docs) still appear in visions — especially in cultures where the name of Jesus is unknown and where the Bible does not exist in the native language. But for us who are blessed to have not only the Bible, but literally thousands of faith-building resources, God usually communicates in less spectacular (though nonetheless supernatural) ways. And though He may not be giving *visions* to many of us, He gives *vision* to all of us — spiritual vision which enables us to look at life through the eyes of faith, to see things from His perspective.

Looking at Life through the Eyes of Faith

Why is it so important for us to have spiritual vision and to be wise stewards of that vision? There are three simple but strategically important reasons:

1. We need vision to find our way on life's journey.

2. We need vision to keep our focus on life's goal.

3. We need vision to set our hearts on life's reward.

> God usually communicates in less spectacular (though nonetheless supernatural) ways. And though He may not be giving **visions** to many of us, He gives **vision** to all of us.

Each one of us is on a journey, trekking through time on a course that begins at a point of God's choosing and ends at a juncture known only to Him. He sees it all from start to finish; yet He longs for us to depend upon Him, to seek His illuminating power as we make our way along the pathway. But God does not reveal His will to us all at once, unrolling it like some sort of cosmic map. He guides us step by step. And sometimes He gives us a vision of what *could* be — a glimpse into a future possibility. That's what David Janney experienced when God flashed that image across his mind — a panoramic, living-color image of one million people gathered in a great plaza listening to a life-changing message. And once God had put that image in his heart, it was up to David to act upon what he had seen. Vision *from* God should lead to action *for* God.

Vision *from* God should lead to action *for* God.

The Importance of Sharing the Vision

One of my colleagues, Glenn Sauls, was serving as pastor of a rapidly growing church in North Carolina when God drew his attention to a parcel of land where the congregation could build a new and much-needed facility. As he stood on the edge of that property for the first time, God enabled Glenn to envision what would one day stand there. It was an epiphanal moment and he knew the vision had to be shared. Over the next weeks, he began to ask key individuals and couples from the church to accompany him to the property. On each occasion, he took folding chairs from the back of his vehicle and invited his guests to sit with him on that unde-veloped land. Then, as they sat in the middle of an open field, Glenn would open his heart and share his vision for the building God would enable them to construct right where they were. Mostly, though, he talked about the lives that would be transformed in that place. Soon, the word began to spread as those who had visited the site began to share the vision with others, encouraging their fellow church members to believe God to make the dream a reality. Of course, that is exactly what happened; and soon a beautiful structure will stand on that property — a vibrant testimony to what happens when God's people steward a vision that He has placed in their hearts.

Spiritual vision is vital to keeping our eyes on life's ultimate goal. We live in the present, but we must be focused on the future, determined to finish well. The apostle Paul put it this way: "But one thing I do: Forgetting what is behind and straining toward what is ahead, I press on toward the goal to win the prize for which God has called me heavenward in Christ Jesus."[9] Our ultimate reward, like our ultimate goal, is not in this life but in the one to come. This is why it is so very important for us to practice the stewardship of vision by "walking in the light as He is in the light."[10] The two most practical ways we can do this are to follow every day the light cast by the lamp of God's Word and to pray unceasingly for spiritually open eyes. We must also remind ourselves constantly that the physical world in which we live is not the ultimate "real" world, that it is not the world which lasts forever.

> Spiritual vision is vital to keeping our eyes on life's ultimate goal. We live in the present, but we must be focused on the future, determined to finish well.

The True Balance of Power

One of the most remarkable stories in the Bible is the account of a conflict between the prophet Elisha and the king of Aram (Syria).[11] In their repeated attempts to attack Israel, the Syrians met with failure after failure because their military plans were known ahead of time. God was revealing the enemy's strategies to Elisha, who was in turn informing the king of Israel. Thinking that he had a traitor in his midst, the king of Syria confronted his officers and demanded to know who was passing along their secret war plans. One of his generals replied, "None of us, my lord the king, but Elisha, the prophet who is in Israel, tells the king of Israel the very words you speak in your bedroom."[12]

> Humanly speaking, the forces on the side of Elisha and his servant were inadequate to meet their foe. What were two unarmed men against an enormous army of soldiers, horses and chariots?

Enraged and bent on revenge, the king of Syria ordered that a huge army be sent to capture the troublesome prophet. A massive contingent of cavalrymen and chariots surrounded the place where Elisha was staying. Early in the morning, his servant went outside and saw the frighteningly large enemy force assembled around them. He cried out to his master, "Oh, my lord, what shall we do?" Elisha replied, "Don't be afraid. Those who are with us are more than those who are with them." And then Elisha prayed, "O Lord, open his eyes so he may see." The Bible tells us that "then the Lord opened the servant's eyes, and he looked and saw the hills full of horses and chariots of fire around Elisha."[13]

Humanly speaking, the forces on the side of Elisha and his servant were inadequate to meet their foe. What were two unarmed men against an enormous army of soldiers, horses and chariots? But, as Zechariah wrote in his prophecy, it is not by human might or power that the child of God is able to win, but by God's Spirit.[14] Our source of strength is not mortal but eternal, and the balance of power is not on the side of the unrighteous. It seemed that the Syrians could easily overwhelm them, but that was based upon physical sight, not spiritual vision. Elisha knew that the balance of power was on his side as he assured his servant, "Those who are with us are more than those who are with them."[15] In fact, the whole Godhead is on the side of the Christian — the Father providentially supplying, the Son interceding on our behalf, the Spirit filling us with His limitless power. God and the believer form a majority.

> God and the believer form a majority.

Seeing the Unseen World

Because God had given him true spiritual vision, Elisha was able to see the spiritual forces protecting them. His servant, once his spiritual eyes had been opened, could also see the angelic army; and he quickly realized that they were vastly superior to the Syrians. For all too many believers (including

Christian leaders), unbelief can be a vision blocker, shutting out spectacular views of the spiritual world.

It is like a cataract on the eyes of the soul. As Paul explained to the Ephesians, the eyes of our understanding must be opened for us to see the realities of an unseen world.[16] And, as he wrote to the Corinthians, we are to look not at the things which are seen, but at the things which are unseen. "For what is seen is temporary, but what is unseen is eternal."[17]

> Unbelief can be a vision blocker, shutting out spectacular views of the spiritual world. It is like a cataract on the eyes of the soul.

Be a wise steward of your God-given vision. Walk in the light as He is in the light. Follow the lamp of His Word. Pray continually for spiritually open eyes. And remember that there is a greater world and a greater reality that He wants you to see as you press toward the mark of your high calling in Jesus Christ.

Scripture References:

1   See Genesis 6:13, 17; 7:4

2   See Genesis 12:1, 2; 15:1-5

3   See Exodus 3:1-10, 16-22

4   See Hebrews 11:7

5   See Hebrews 11:8-12

6   See Hebrews 11:24-29

7   John 16:13-14

8   Hebrews 13:8

9   Philippians 3:13-14

10 See 1 John 1:7

11 See 2 Kings 6:8-23

12 2 Kings 6:12

13 See 2 Kings 6:15-17

14 See Zechariah 4:6

15 2 Kings 6:16

16 See Ephesians 1:18

17 2 Corinthians 4:18

THE
STEWARDSHIP
OF
INFLUENCE

CHAPTER 2

THE STEWARDSHIP OF INFLUENCE

Prominently displayed in the Pro Football Hall of Fame in Canton, Ohio, is a life-size bronze bust of Don Shula, legendary head coach of the Baltimore Colts and the Miami Dolphins. Visitors study Shula's rugged features on that sculpture as they read the plaque which recounts his impressive accomplishments. When he concluded his 33rd and final season in 1995, Don Shula was the winningest head coach in NFL history. His teams won the Super Bowl twice; and his 1972 Dolphins achieved the only perfect season ever, finishing with a 17-0 record.

For 11 memorable seasons I had the extraordinary privilege of serving as Chaplain to the Miami Dolphins football team. During those years I had a front-row seat (actually, a sideline bench) that enabled me to see up-close and personal one of the most gifted coaches of our generation — of any generation, in fact. For me, the essence of Don Shula is not captured in a bronze statue or a highlight film, but in the man I observed for those 11 seasons. I count Don Shula as a friend and a gentle-man; but I will always think of him foremost as a leader of men. In conversations with him and in observations of him, I learned so much about the stewardship of influence.

Recently I had a conversation with Lyle Blackwood, who played strong safety on the Dolphins team that went to Super Bowl XIX. We were discussing those exciting days and I asked Lyle what stood out most for him when he thought of Shula's leadership. Lyle replied, "The thing that I admired most about Coach Shula was how much he loved the game and how focused he was when we were in the heat of battle. He was on the field with the players all of the time, in mind and spirit, always using every ounce of influence he had. To be a good coach you have to feel like that — to be one with the players and with what is going on in the game. You have to be so connected to the game that, even though you are on the sideline, your players are an extension of you and you play through them. I believe that's why Coach got so into the game and didn't mind giving us a piece of his mind on many occasions. He took it personally because he felt like he was on the field with us."

When Lyle shared that, I remembered that Don Shula could be a very difficult man when he was pushing his players to excel. But one phrase in Lyle's comments captures the reason Coach Shula was like that: he was "using every ounce of influ-ence he had" to get the greatest possible result from his teams.

The stewardship of influence may seem at first glance like a topic that fits only a select percentage of people, but the fact is that every person exercises influence. The sphere of that influence can differ measurably from one person to another, but each of us is influential in very definable ways. How we use and manage our influence can spell the difference between success and failure, for us and for those whose lives we affect.

We first learn about influence through a mother's soothing voice and warm embrace. Whatever she says or does affects how we feel and what we think. Through her we experience virtually everything that is foundational to life itself. In her sphere of influence, no one is more important; and we sense it even in our infancy. As one grows older, a mother's influence changes; but it is always there, for good or bad. Some mothers unfortunately cannot bring themselves to adapt wisely to the changes that time and maturity demand. They keep on mothering in a way that fails to properly utilize their influence. Dr. James Dobson tells the story of a friend whose mother had the wisdom to recognize the evolving nature of her influence. After his first hectic week at college, Dobson's friend received a package from home. It was a large, nondescript envelope that contained a strangely shaped object. With great curiosity the young man hurriedly opened the package. Inside

> The stewardship of influence may seem at first glance like a topic that fits only a select percentage of people, but the fact is that every person exercises influence.

was a pair of neatly starched, ironed and folded apron strings. Mom had cut them off and sent them as a symbolic, loving acknowledgement of her son's newfound independence. What a brilliant woman!

In essence, the stewardship of influence is the stewardship of relationships. Your life may have an impact in some field of endeavor; but ultimately and most significantly, your influence affects other people. And this is as it should be because it is what truly matters. As a friend once told me with great intensity, "Kirk, only two things last forever — the Word of God and the souls of human beings." I have never forgotten those words, and I hope I never do. They have challenged me to keep my focus on things eternal — driving me right to the core issue of how I steward the influence God has given me.

> Your life may have an impact in some field of endeavor, but ultimately and most significantly, your influence affects other people.

As I see it, for a Christian there are three primary objectives at stake in the stewardship of influence; and these govern how one should live. The faithful steward is committed to…

1. Influencing people to know the One True God.

2. Influencing people to believe in and follow Jesus Christ.

3. Influencing people to live a normal Christian life.

The practical outworking of these three purposes is a lifelong challenge, but it is infinitely, immeasurably rewarding.

Influencing People to Know the One True God

It is becoming increasingly unpopular in our secularized culture to suggest that there is one true God. A lot of people get nervous when they hear such a statement because it implies that there are numerous false gods that are being worshiped. And, as is commonly thought, it's just not nice to say bad things about somebody else's god. However, if there is indeed only one true God, and He has revealed Himself definitively and has confirmed His uniqueness absolutely, we must proclaim it to everyone.

If there is indeed only one true God, and He has revealed Himself definitively and has confirmed His uniqueness absolutely, we must proclaim it to everyone.

Who is the one true God and what can we say about Him?

He is the God of the Bible. Penned by more than 40 writers on three continents over the span of 1,500 years, the Bible is the Book of Books. By its own testimony, it is the very word of God, an inspired expression of His truth and His character. The Bible does not merely *contain* the words of God, as some contend; it *is* the Word of God; and in its authoritative message God communicates what we need to know about Him and how we ought to live for Him.

He is Creator and Lord of All. The very first verse of the Bible says, "In the beginning, God created the heavens and the earth."[1] By His command, the universe was spoken into existence. Out of nothing He brought forth everything. This planet and all that it contains was created by Him, and it is all subject to His lordship. "For by him all things were created: things in heaven and on earth, visible and invisible, whether thrones or powers or rulers or authorities; all things were created by him and for him. He is before all things, and in him all things hold together."[2]

He is the Eternal Triune God. In a way that we cannot begin to grasp because it is so far beyond our comprehension, God is three Persons in One. He is God the Father, God the Son and God the Holy Spirit; yet He is One God. When we refer to any or all of these Persons, we are referring to God Himself, not to some concept about Him. We see His plurality from the very start of the Scriptures when God said, "Let *us* make man in *our* image...."[3] And we see His triune nature at the baptism of Jesus when the Father speaks His approval, the Son demonstrates His obedience to the Father, and the Spirit comes in confirmation of the divine will.[4]

He is the One and Only Savior of Mankind. The Gospel of John says that the Father so loved sinful mankind that He gave His "only begotten Son" so that we might receive eternal life through Him.[5] That wonderful phrase from the King James version — "only begotten Son" — means that He was the one and only, the unique one who was fully man and yet fully God. He would make salvation possible through His perfect life, sacrificial death and victorious resurrection. God's desire is that we as flawed, sinful human beings, who are incapable of saving ourselves, would put our trust in the person and work of Jesus Christ, the Son of God.

Influencing People to Believe in and Follow Jesus Christ

It's one thing to say that there is one true God. But it's quite another thing to say that there is only one way to know Him. As Christians, that *is* what we say. Not because we are arrogant or narrow-minded, or because we hold to an antiquated way of thinking. We aren't arrogant, because arrogance is based upon ignorant pride that draws attention to self, as opposed to this belief, which directs attention to God. We aren't narrow-minded, because narrow-minded-ness implies a petty and limited range of vision, as opposed to this belief that sees the whole breadth of nature created by one eternal Being. And we don't follow an antiquated way of thinking because that implies that the belief is an obsolete concept, out-moded and discredited as opposed to this belief that is still relevant and even transformational today.

> It's one thing to say that there is one true God. But it's quite another thing to say that there is only one way to know Him. As Christians, that *is* what we say.

We say as Christians that there is only one way to God because that's what the Bible says: "Salvation is found in no one else, for there is no other name under heaven given to men by which we must be saved."[6] This is a categorical statement that leaves no room whatsoever for flexibility or alternative ideas. If one wants to receive eternal salvation, there is no one else who can give it except Jesus. There is no other name but His name with the authority to give life and give it abundantly. Jesus said to His disciples, "I am the way and the truth and the life. No one comes to the Father except through me."[7]

> We are called to communicate to everyone within our sphere of influence that Jesus is the way, the truth and the life.

We are called to communicate to everyone within our sphere of influence that Jesus is the way, the truth and the life. As His followers, we spread this good news and we witness to the reality of our life in Him. I can tell you without reservation that I have experienced no greater feeling than the joy of leading someone to Christ and seeing that person spiritually transformed.

While working on this very chapter, God gave me a marvelous opportunity to share my faith. In a very unusual place, I was able to practice the stewardship of influence as I told someone God's plan of salvation. It happened on a hunting trip near Mt. McKinley, North America's tallest mountain. McKinley, which soars over 20,000 feet into the Alaskan sky, is called Denali by the native tribes. It is a spectacular sight from any perspective, and we had a great view of the mountain from our campsite about 40 miles west of the peak.

Our party was led by two highly experienced hunting guides — great outdoorsmen who are passionate about their work and remarkable in their skill at guiding hunts for mountain sheep, moose and brown bears. I listened with great fascination to their stories of adventure in the wilds of Alaska. When one of them asked me, "Kirk, what do you do for a living?" the whole experience changed instantly for me from hunting expedition to fishing trip. I say that because when someone asks me what I do, I always take it as an opportunity to be, as Jesus said, a "fisher of men."[8] I told those two burly men how a pastor took the time to come by my house when I was 12 years old to tell me the meaning of John 3:16. I described how he unfolded the truth of that verse which says, "For God so loved the world that he gave his only begotten son, that whosoever believes in him shall not perish but have everlasting life." I recounted how he told me that the word "whosoever" included me. As I went on with my story it was clear that the message was connecting with one of those two men. It was exactly what he had been waiting to hear all his life. Before the trip was over, he had put his faith in Jesus Christ. I look back to that and think, Man, what could be better than being in Alaska on a hunting trip with the opportunity to fish for men!

In the stewardship of influence, the making of disciples is imperative. It is something we absolutely, positively must do. Jesus said emphatically, "Go...and make disciples of all nations..."[9] This statement is not a recommendation or a suggestion.

It is a command of our Lord to His followers of all generations. And, according to John's Gospel, when we obey this command, we show that we are true disciples of Christ.[10] Disciple making is not synonymous with evangelism, but begins with evangelism. First, a person is led to faith in Christ; then that person is led to follow Christ. Leading someone to faith in Christ is evangelism. Leading someone to follow Christ wholeheartedly is disciple making. The process of discipleship begins the instant one trusts in Jesus as Lord and Savior, and it continues throughout a believer's life. To make a disciple is to guide a new or immature believer to spiritual maturity. It involves these essentials:

"Go...and make disciples of all nations..." This statement is not a recommendation or a suggestion. It is a command of our Lord to His followers of all generations.

Equipping them with the Word of God. To grow in Christ one must grow in the Word. Writing on this subject, Paul advised the Colossians, "Let the word of Christ dwell in you richly as you teach and admonish one another with all wisdom."[11] When he gave his final good-bye to the elders at Ephesus — men he had personally discipled — Paul said, "I have not hesitated to proclaim to you the whole will of God."[12] He had communicated to them a full and adequate understanding of God's Word and God's will. This is our priority in making disciples today as we impart the truths of Scripture to others so that they might mature in their faith.

Engaging them in sharing their faith. One of the most natural activities for a new believer is to share the life-transforming truth that he or she has discovered. This was the response of Andrew, one of the first disciples. The Bible says, "Andrew, Simon Peter's brother, was one of the two who heard what John had said and who had followed Jesus. The first thing Andrew did was to find his brother Simon and tell him, 'We have found the Messiah' (that is, the Christ). Then he brought Simon to Jesus."[13] Even as a brand-new, fledgling disciple, Andrew was already evangelizing, already sharing his faith. This is exactly as it should be. Courses and classes in personal evangelism are often helpful, but most important of all is that believers actually evangelize. There is no substitute for sharing one's faith, because each personal testimony is unique and powerful. When you tell how God has transformed your life, there is nothing anyone can say to disagree or refute your witness.

> When you tell how God has transformed your life, there is nothing anyone can say to disagree or refute your witness.

That's how it was for a blind man who was healed by Jesus. When he was called before the religious authorities he told them, "One thing I do know. I was blind but now I see!"[14] I urge you, use your influence to tell the story of your own spiritual journey and to engage others in doing likewise.

Encouraging them to steward their lives for the glory of God. When we understand that the purpose of life is to serve God and bring Him glory, it motivates us to encourage other believers — especially new believers — to invest their lives in fulfilling the same purpose. In Christ we have a newness of life that results in new ways of thinking, feeling, speaking and acting. His Spirit within us is the enabling power to break old habits and form new patterns of behavior. As we become more aware of His Word and more conscious of His will, we grow stronger in the faith. With the increase in our own spiritual maturity we can have increasing influence in the lives of other people. This leads us directly to the third objective.

> No one expects nor can anyone reach perfection; but we can attain balance, and this is central to making the most of your impact upon others.

Influencing People to Live a Normal Christian Life

If Jesus is your Savior and Lord, in all of your relationships — whether to family, friends, acquaintances or others — you are a witness for Him. By what you do and say, by how you act and react, by the attitudes you display, others will see Him either honored or dishonored. It is inevitable that, positively or negatively, you will affect the lives of other people. The most important concern then is how to ensure that your influence is positive. No one expects nor can anyone reach perfection; but we can attain balance, and this is central to making the most of your impact upon others. This was an essential idea set forth by Watchman Nee, a leader of the church in China who died as a martyr in

1972. In his profoundly challenging way, Nee urged believers to live a "normal Christian life" — one that is spiritually whole and balanced. As he explained, balance implies the spiritual steadiness that comes from walking with Christ and running the race of faith. The balance that others observe in you is not physical steadiness but spiritual equilibrium, which is expressed in balanced thinking, emotions, speech and actions. What they see in your life can inspire others to replicate in their own lives. Let's consider each of these four areas:

Influencing how others think. The well-balanced Christian thinks clearly and positively. Thinking clearly means maintaining the right view of God, of self and of life situations. This facilitates wise decision making and correct judgment about the big things in life as well as the minor. Thinking positively is a matter of looking for and finding the good even when everything may seem bad. It also means focusing on solutions as well as problems. Negative thinkers can have a damaging and even destructive effect upon those around them because negativity by its very nature pulls down rather than builds up. Exercising his influence with the Philippians, the apostle Paul gave them very specific instructions that we, too, should heed: "Finally, brothers, whatever is true, whatever is noble, whatever is right, whatever is pure, whatever is lovely, whatever is admirable—if anything is excellent or praiseworthy—think about such things."[15]

> Thinking clearly means maintaining the right view of God, of self and of life situations.

Influencing how others feel. Every person (including, of course, all the people within your sphere of influence) wants to feel appreciated and feel affirmed. This is true not just of Christians but also of every human being. The right use of influence can evoke these important feelings. By communicating healthy praise and honest gratitude to others, you magnify their sense of true worth. And when you communicate genuine acceptance and admiration, the other person feels affirmed. "Let your way of life be always seasoned with salt," says Colossians 4:6. Salt is a preservative that keeps things from spoiling — including relationships. As an influencer, live in a way that is loving and graceful, never corrupt. People are watching you, and your behavior has the potential to make them feel positive about Jesus Christ and be drawn to Him or to feel negative and be driven away from Him.

Influencing how others speak. As the book of James states so emphatically, the words we speak have tremendous power. They can warm another person's heart or shatter it to pieces. They can hurt or heal. Words, in fact, can often hurt far more than deeds. Words of rejection can destroy a person's spirit, but words of encouragement can lift the spirit and make it soar. James 3:3-4 compares the influence of words to the way a horse is restrained by the bit and bridle and the way a ship is controlled by a small rudder. In the exercise of influence, what you say must be careful and constructive in order to promote the same kind of carefulness and constructiveness in the person whom you influence.

Influencing how others act. The old adage says that actions speak louder than words, and this is true in the sense that actions are physically observed while words are mentally absorbed. Ideally, there should be no conflict between your actions and your words as you practice the stewardship of influence. When you act responsibly and wisely, those whom you influence can see your example and follow it. That was Paul's strategy in making disciples among the Corinthians when he told them to imitate his way of life. He wrote to them, "Follow my example, as I follow the example of Christ."[16] He wasn't asking them to be *his* disciples, but to be *Christ's* disciples in the same way that he was. Through his exemplary influence they would learn to act prudently and with true spiritual confidence.

Have you ever wondered where your English Bible came from? Have you ever been curious as to who was most instrumental in translating the ancient Scriptures into our modern English language?

When I think of a truly influential Christian many people come to mind, but at the top of the list I would have to put William Tyndale. Though he lived hundreds of years ago, his life and his work affect us every day. In case you don't believe me, let me pose a couple of questions: Have you ever wondered where your English Bible came from? Have you ever been curious as to who was most instrumental in translating the ancient Scriptures into our modern English language? The answer to those important questions is discovered in one extraordinary man, William Tyndale. More than any other person in the past 500 years, Tyndale shaped not only our English Bible but our English language as well. Talk about influence!

William Tyndale was born in England sometime between 1490 and 1495. In 1510 he began his theological studies at Oxford. Eleven years later, in 1521, Tyndale was ordained to the priesthood and began preaching widely. In the first year of his public ministry, Tyndale spoke out against corruption within the Church and was accused of being a heretic. But he was most burdened by the fact that there was no Bible in the English language, so he resolved to translate the Scriptures.

When Tyndale made his solemn decision to put the words of the Bible into his own language, his fate was sealed. It was illegal to do such a thing in England. Under constant pressure and threats against his life, Tyndale journeyed to Germany to enlist the assistance of Martin Luther, who was then working on a translation of the Bible into German. With Luther's encouragement, Tyndale worked tirelessly to produce his first English edition of the New Testament. But his secret project was discovered and Tyndale was forced to flee to Cologne. In that city as well he encountered opposition and the Senate of Cologne voted to prohibit him from printing and distributing his unlawful work.

From Cologne, William Tyndale traveled to the city of Worms, where he completed the translation and printing of the first edition of the English New Testament in 1525. Brave messengers smuggled those historic new books into England, but nearly every copy was seized and burned. Of the 3,000 that were produced, only three remain, and only one of those is complete. The Archbishop of Canterbury, William Warham, took the extraordinary step of buying numerous copies before they reached England for the express purpose of burning them himself. When the news of Tyndale's scandalous translation was made public, a warrant was issued and the authorities in Worms attempted to arrest him. He escaped moments before they arrived.

On the run but always at work, Tyndale continued to translate the Scriptures. Friends and associates urged him to return to England, but Tyndale feared hostility from the ecclesiastical authorities and remained on the Continent in order to finish his breakthrough work. In 1535, Tyndale was betrayed by a friend and was captured and imprisoned in Vilvorde Castle, the state prison near Brussels.

> On the run but always at work, Tyndale continued to translate the Scriptures.

Despite the appeals of influential English merchants and the royal adviser, Thomas Cromwell, Tyndale was tried and convicted of heresy. He was sentenced to die for his "crimes." Having offended Henry VIII, the king made no effort to intercede on Tyndale's behalf. On October 6, 1536, William Tyndale was garroted and his body then burned at the stake. His last words were, "Lord, open the King of England's eyes."

Though his greatest work was produced while he was in exile from his native land, Tyndale was the most influential figure of the English Reformation. His writings shaped the thought of the Puritans and his translation of the Bible essentially created the modern English language. Tyndale's work formed the basis of the famed Authorized Version, the King James Bible of 1611, which incorporated over 91% of his work. Literally thousands of the words and phrases which have become commonplace in the English language to this very day originated with Tyndale's translation of the Scriptures. It is often said that William Shakespeare's phraseology influenced the making of the King James Bible. Actually, this is not true, for it was Tyndale who first influenced Shakespeare. Scholars have now recorded over 5,000 instances in which William Shakespeare used the wording, syntax and phrasing of William Tyndale!

> Scholars have now recorded over 5,000 instances in which Shakespeare used the wording, syntax and phrasing of William Tyndale!

The next time someone asks you where your English Bible came from, tell them that it came through the God-blessed work of a man who stewarded his influence in a way that made history — the father of our modern English language, the incomparable William Tyndale.

Scripture References:

1   Genesis 1:1

2   Colossians 1:16-17

3   Genesis 1:26

4   See Matthew 3:16-17; Mark 1:9-11; Luke 3:21-22; John 1:29-34

5   See John 3:16 (KJV)

6   Acts 4:12

7   John 14:6

8   See Matthew 4:19; Mark 1:17

9   See Matthew 28:19

10   John 15:8

11   Colossians 3:16

12   Acts 20:27

13   John 1:40-42

14   John 9:25

15   Philippians 4:8

16   1 Corinthians 11:1

THE
STEWARDSHIP
OF
COMMITMENT

CHAPTER 3

THE STEWARDSHIP OF COMMITMENT

There were a lot of people who didn't want him to make the trip, but Franklin Graham knew that he had to go. As president of the international Christian relief organization, Samaritan's Purse, Graham had decided to make a perilous visit to strife-ridden Sudan in northern Africa. Torn by years of conflict, Sudan is a desperately needy place where millions have fallen victim to widespread genocide and war-induced famine. Arab tribesmen from the predominantly Islamic north have been slaughtering black Africans in the historically Christian regions in the south of Sudan. It is a race war that is one of this decade's most horrendous, hate-driven struggles. Samaritan's Purse operates a field hospital in southern Sudan that has come under increasing pressures in spite of its neutrality as a medical center. The hospital grounds had been bombed seven times by Muslim forces, missing the building but killing numerous people in the area; so Graham decided to visit Sudan's President Omar Al-Bashir, a Muslim whose own government was behind the bombings. "You shouldn't go, they will cut your head off!" Graham said he had been warned. But he answered, "No, I am going and I'm going to be a witness."

When Franklin Graham arrived in Sudan he met with a number of different groups, including a delegation of mullahs that were giving spiritual direction to President Al-Bashir. Graham also met with Christians who were living under the severest persecution. He encouraged them to stay strong in the faith, and then he went to meet the Sudanese president. Al-Bashir speaks English; but because Graham did not want there to be any misunderstandings, he took along Sammy Daghar, a leading pastor from Lebanon, to be his translator. After pleasantries were exchanged, Graham said, "Mr. President, I want you to know that I have been working in your country for a number of years in the south, and I have a hospital." The president turned to one of his aides and said, "Didn't we bomb that hospital?" The aide answered, "Yes," and Al-Bashir looked back at Graham smiling and laughing. Franklin Graham replied, "Yes, Mr. President. And you missed." Al-Bashir quit laughing. Then he said, "I want to make you a Muslim." Graham replied, "Really? I would love to give you a chance to make me a Muslim. I'd love to give you that opportunity to try, because I want to win you to faith in Jesus Christ." The president was taken aback and Graham said, "I want to come to your country and I want to preach from one end of your nation to the other in freedom. The Christians in your country don't want more rights than Muslims. They just want the same rights. We want the right to preach, just like you have the right to preach when you come to America. Muslims can come and they can preach with freedom and we want the same rights in the Sudan, which we don't have. We want the same freedom not only to preach but to proselytize and to build churches without the interference and per-secution of the government."

Al-Bashir replied, "I think some of the problems we have had with the church have been because of the war. And if peace comes maybe we will have that kind of relationship with the church." Rather than countering that statement, Franklin Graham began to present the Gospel to the president. "I told him I believed in Jesus Christ as God's Son. I told him I believe He died for the sins of all men, and that He was raised from the dead and that He's coming back again. And I said that if we put our faith and trust in Jesus Christ, God will forgive us of our sins."

"I want to come to your country and I want to preach from one end of your nation to the other in freedom. The Christians in your country don't want more rights than Muslims. They just want the same rights."

After having heard such a bold witness for Christ right in the center of his presidential headquarters, Al-Bashir sat passively for some time, looking Franklin Graham squarely in the face. A few moments later, the meeting was adjourned and Graham and Sammy Daghar left for their other obligations. However, immediately afterward, the government of Sudan informed Samaritan's Purse that they would be free to work unimpeded in any area of the country!

Graham commented recently, "I spoke through the translation of Sammy Daghar, because I knew that if I didn't make the Gospel clear, Sammy would make it very clear. And if I messed up, I knew Sammy would catch it. I had been critical of Al-Bashir, and I have not backed off my criticism. But when you are a witness for Christ, God will bless your efforts. When you stand up for Christ, Jesus Christ will stand up for you and He will guide you, He will direct you. He will never leave you, He will never forsake you. But we are to be witnesses — even to people we despise and people we don't like."

> "When you stand up for Christ, Jesus Christ will stand up for you and He will guide you, He will direct you. He will never leave you, He will never forsake you. But we are to be witnesses — even to people we despise and people we don't like."

While they were still in Khartoum, Sammy Daghar was asked to speak to a church in the area. Franklin gave his blessing and Sammy agreed to go. Prior to the meeting, Sammy asked the pastor if there were any Muslim informers in the congregation. He replied, "Oh, yes. They are here every Sunday. But you go ahead and you preach the Gospel. They have already killed so many of us, let them kill some more. What difference does it make? You preach the Gospel!" Later, Pastor Daghar said, "That had a tremendous impact on me. I had never heard anybody speak like that. I went back to my own country of Lebanon even more committed and even stronger in my witness for Jesus Christ."

The Christians of Sudan were ready and willing to give everything — even their lives — so that God's liberating truth could be proclaimed in their country. It is very difficult for us in the relative comforts of North America to comprehend what our Christian brothers and sisters in many other nations must deal with every day. But the fact is that all of us, wherever we are and whatever our circumstances, make commitments for the sake of Christ. And, once we have made a commitment — whether small or large — we must steward it for the glory and purposes of God.

> All of us, wherever we are and whatever our circumstances, make commitments for the sake of Christ.

The stewardship of commitment extends to every role, every responsibility and every important relationship. And for the Christian, commitment has an even deeper significance because it is the evidence of genuine loyalty to Christ. Jesus said to His disciples, "A new command I give you: Love one another. As I have loved you, so you must love one another. All men will know that you are my disciples, if you love one another."[1] The central identifying characteristic of a Christian is commitment demonstrated through love. Christians aren't supposed to be spotted by their W.W.J.D. bracelets, their gold crosses or their clever bumper stickers. There is a better identifier: consistent, committed, Christ-like love.

What does this mean in the most practical terms? How can you as a believer be an effective steward of life's commitments? Let me suggest that a wise approach focuses on three areas in particular: your commitment to *people*, your commitment to *prayer* and your commitment to *principles*.

Stewarding Your Commitment to People

One of the best sources on this subject is Paul's letter to the Philippians. In the four brief chapters of his epistle we find a treasure trove filled with insights into the meaning of committed relationships. As he wrote his deeply personal letter, Paul was incarcerated in the dark isolation of a Roman prison. Yet in that depressing place, the great apostle had the encouraging influence of happy memories. He thought back to Philippi and his mind overflowed with joyous remembrances of what God had done in so many lives in that strategic city. In the first part of the first chapter, Paul shares something of what the memories meant to him. His heartfelt words instruct us in the ways we can steward our relationships with people in general and with our Christian brothers and sisters in particular.

Be thankful for people. Paul writes, "I thank my God every time I remember you."[2] Rather than feel sorry for himself (as many of us do when we're in dire circumstances), he thought of the Philippian Christians and thanked God for them. Actually, he had several reasons to scold them; but he set those things aside and gave thanks for all that was praiseworthy in them. Paul's thankfulness was directed to

God, because He was the one who had made their relationship possible. His feelings were prompted by a heart full of loving gratitude.

Think of the people in your life — loved ones who are closest to you, extended family members, friends, acquaintances, classmates, co-workers, team-mates, neighbors and others. God has blessed you with the opportunity to know each one, to learn from them, to share with them, to experience the ups and downs of life with them. Thank Him for those people with consistent appreciation.

Be thoughtful of people. Every time that Paul remembered his friends at Philippi, he was spiritually and emotionally joined with them once again.[3] Though physically separated by a great distance, he was with them in a very real way. For most of us, memories fade. Even some of the most sensitive relationships are all too soon forgotten: childhood friends...high school buddies...close neighbors...and often we can't even remember their names! Paul held the Philippians in his heart and mind and he simply would not let his memories fade. Some of the things that happened to Paul in Philippi could have produced sorrow — his illegal arrest, the beating he received, his discomfort in prison — but even those things brought joyous recollections of the relationships he had established.

> Relationships are all too soon forgotten: childhood friends... high school buddies ...close neighbors... and often we can't even remember their names!

Being thoughtful means putting the interests of others before your own interests, having the heart of a servant just as Jesus did. It means truly listening and truly caring in every way that is reasonably possible. And when you pray for others, be specific and focused, interceding just as Paul did for the Philippians whenever he was away from them.

Be trustworthy with people. The foundation of strong human relationships is trust. If there is no trust there can be no viable connection or communication. Marriages fall apart when trust is broken. Businesses crumble when partners violate their agreements. Wars are launched when nations go against the treaties they once signed. Trust is vital and trustworthiness is imperative at all levels of society. As Christians we have a unique understanding of this because trust is the basis of our relationship to God: we place our faith (our full trust) in the person and work of Christ. And, because we believe in Him and belong to Him, we have the potential of an even deeper relationship with one another as His children. Our "partnership in the Gospel,"[4] as Paul called it, transcends all kinds of barriers, enabling people from radically different backgrounds to share a spiritual bond that is indescribable. I have traveled around the world and visited dozens of nations, and wherever I have met fellow Christians I am profoundly conscious of the real meaning of "partnership in the Gospel." There is a connection, and there is communication; and it is very special.

> Relationships must be cultivated and maintained; they don't simply happen (even among Christians).

To be trustworthy is to be one on whom others can depend. In the stewardship of your commitment to people this is paramount. So, keep your promises, honor your word and do what is right. Relationships must be cultivated and maintained; they don't simply happen (even among Christians). Don't wait for others to take the initiative and then complain that people don't really care for you! Be proactive and be determined to make the most of every opportunity to connect with those whom God brings along the pathway of your life. Don't miss what He has in store for you.

When I began to think about this subject of stewarding a commitment to people, the first person who came to mind was Faye Gordon. I'm sure you have never heard of Faye because she isn't famous and she has never sought attention or acclaim. When I pastored a rapidly growing church in Miami, Faye Gordon had the responsibility of directing our nursery. On Easter Sunday one year, Faye came to me in tears and said, "Pastor, we are overwhelmed with babies! Please, please expand our facilities!" Of course, we responded to her emotional (but very reasonable) request, because everyone knew that she cared for those precious children as if they were her own. Since sometime in the 1950s she had faithfully served week after week, stewarding her commitment to the littlest people in our very large congregation.

Whether she was gently rocking a newborn, singing a song or quoting Bible verses to a cooing child, Faye Gordon showed a tenderness and care that still brings a smile to my face. She was also a great source of wisdom to first-time mothers, giving each one a feeling of much-needed confidence. In 1994, Faye retired from the nursery after nearly four decades of changing diapers and changing lives. Because of her faithfulness in stewarding her commitment, parents were able to hear the Gospel, couples were able to worship together, and thousands of children were blessed by the gentleness of an exceptional woman. On the day she retired, we had a special service, celebrating her life with roses and gifts and recognition. Without prompting, the entire church rose in a huge, sustained standing ovation. It was a fitting tribute to a lady whose Christ-like spirit showed all of us how devotion can make such a difference.

> What a profound, mysterious thing prayer is: our personal means of communication with the One who spoke the worlds into existence.

Stewarding Your Commitment to Prayer

It would be impossible for me to overemphasize the importance of prayer. No spiritual activity is greater in significance or in consequence, or more relevant to the matter of stewardship. I have no idea how many sermons I have preached and lessons I have taught on the subject of prayer, yet I am certain that I've barely scratched the surface! What a profound, mysterious thing prayer is: our personal means of communication with the One who spoke the worlds into existence. Where do we begin to explore this priceless spiritual privilege that God has given us? The answer that comes most readily to mind is to look first to Jesus. What did He say about prayer that can equip us for stewarding this vital commitment?

Luke 11:1 says, "One day Jesus was praying in a certain place. When he finished, one of his disciples said to him, 'Lord, teach us to pray, just as John taught his disciples.'" This disciple, whoever he was, had observed the prayer life of Jesus and he made one of the most important requests any believer can put before the Lord: Teach us to pray. What a wise request, because effectiveness in the Christian life is inseparably connected to one's effectiveness in prayer. Prayer is an absolute necessity, for it is to the spiritual dimension what breathing is to the physical. How long could you manage without breathing?

> Effectiveness in the Christian life is inseparably connected to one's effectiveness in prayer.

Fortunately, Jesus answered the disciple's request. In Matthew's Gospel we read a fuller account of what He said:

"This, then, is how you should pray:
'Our Father in heaven, hallowed be your name,
your kingdom come, your will be done
on earth as it is in heaven.
Give us today our daily bread.
Forgive us our debts, as we also have forgiven our
  debtors.
And lead us not into temptation, but deliver us
  from the evil one.'"[5]

This is often called "the Lord's Prayer," although a more appropriate term would be "the Disciple's Prayer" since it is a pattern intended to teach us how to pray in the will of God. It is a mistake to think of this prayer as something that must be constantly repeated, as if there is a certain blessing received each time you recite it. This prayer is a model for us to follow, not a form for us to recite. Constant repetition of prayer can become an empty ritual, like some kind of rosary, minus the beads.

Pray to the Father. "Our Father" is such a rich, two-fold expression. As I read this phrase, the word "Our" reminds me of the relationship that I share with other Christians, and the word "Father" reminds me of my relationship to God. Notice that this model prayer contains no personal pronouns in the singular form. This is a family prayer, involving the Father in heaven and His children on earth. As members of this family we must want what the Father wants because His name is "hallowed" — it is holy and honored. Prayer, rightly so, starts with respect for the Father, not the requests of the Father's children. This is why it is so beneficial to begin a dedicated time of prayer with praise to God for who He is, our loving and gracious Father.

Pray for God's kingdom to come and His will to be done. We are to pray that God's kingdom would come and that His will would be done. His desire must be our desire; and if it is any other way, we are the ones who need realignment. Anything in my praying that does not advance God's kingdom or glorify His name is against His will. We must not lose sight of the fact that Jesus came for one purpose only: to do the will of the Father. He reminded the disciples of this repeatedly because He wanted them to understand that it was their purpose as well — as it is for us as disciples today.

Pray for needs to be met. God's concerns take precedence over our concerns. As we grow in spiritual maturity and learn more of what it means to seek first the kingdom of God and His righteousness, our requests in prayer change. The Lord is concerned about the needs we have, but He wants us to see those needs in the context of higher purposes. Because He loves us, He will provide for us, meeting our needs day by day. In the Sermon on the Mount, Jesus said, "Ask and it will be given to you; seek, and you will find; knock and the door will be opened to you. For everyone who asks receives; he who seeks finds; and to him who knocks, the door will be opened."[6] Then He concludes with an illustration and a phenomenal promise: "Which of you, if his son asks for bread, will give him a stone? Or if he asks for a fish, will give him a snake? If you, then, though you are evil, know how to give good gifts to your children, how much more will your Father in heaven give good gifts to those who ask him!"[7] From His eternal riches He will faithfully supply our "daily bread" and meet all of our needs.

> We must not lose sight of the fact that Jesus came for one purpose only: to do the will of the Father. He reminded the disciples of this repeatedly because He wanted them to understand that it was their purpose as well.

Pray for forgiveness. To pray, "Forgive us our debts…" is similar to praying, "Forgive us our sins…." The word translated "debt" in our English Bible refers to an obligation that has been incurred, either by a sin of omission or commission. For these obligations to be "forgiven" is for them to be cancelled. The emphasis in this part of the Lord's Prayer is on the necessity of our forgiving one another. This verse is not referring to the forgiveness that leads to salvation, but the forgiveness that leads to harmony within the family of God. If we are not forgiving toward one another we cannot live in fellowship with one another or with the Lord. But, thankfully, as John wrote in his first epistle, "If we confess our sins, he is faithful and just and will forgive us our sins and purify us from all unrighteousness."[8]

> Prayer is a great privilege that demands a deep commitment, a commitment that must be stewarded with wisdom and care.

Pray for deliverance. The concluding phrase of Christ's model prayer says, "And lead us not into temptation, but deliver us from the evil one." This temporal world in which we live is under the influence of Satan and his demonic agents. He is "the evil one" to whom this prayer refers, and it is from him that we pray to be delivered. As long as we live in this world we will be subjected to temptations and trials, but God will enable us to resist and withstand whatever comes against us. The battle in which we are engaged is a spiritual conflict, and His interventions gives us a spiritual deliverance. As Paul wrote to the Corinthians, " For though we live in the world, we do not wage war as the world does. The weapons we fight with are not the weapons of the world. On the contrary, they have divine power to demolish strongholds."[9]

Prayer is a great privilege that demands a deep commitment, a commitment that must be stewarded with wisdom and care. I urge you: Pray unceasingly, pray expectantly and pray earnestly. As James put it, the prayer of a righteous person "is powerful and effective."[10]

Stewarding Your Commitment to Principles

In the spring of 1990, Bill McCartney, then football coach for the University of Colorado, was traveling to a banquet in southern Colorado with his friend, Dr. Dave Wardell. In their conversation along the way, Coach McCartney asked Dave, "What do you feel is the most important factor in changing a man spiritually, from immaturity to maturity?" Dr. Wardell instantly replied, "Discipleship." Bill then began to share his vision of a stadium filled with 50,000 men, coming together for an extraordinary event devoted to learning what it means to be a disciple of Jesus Christ. In his mind's eye he saw those tens of thousands gathered at the University's Folsom Field, encouraging, inspiring and gaining strength from one another. As he described his

> Coach McCartney asked Dave, "What do you feel is the most important factor in changing a man spiritually, from immaturity to maturity?" Dr. Wardell instantly replied, "Discipleship."

dream to his friend, Coach McCartney said that he believed that such a meeting could spark a spiritual awakening and result in a deepening of discipleship among men nationwide.

The vision that was shared that day became the impetus for a movement which has become much broader in scope than Bill McCartney, Dave Wardell or anyone else ever imagined. It was the birth of what is now known as Promise Keepers. "Way back before Promise Keepers had a name," says Coach McCartney, "we looked up the word *integrity* in *Webster's Dictionary*. He gave six definitions: 'utter sincerity, honesty, candor, not artificial, not shallow, no empty promises.'" For a group totally committed to Christ, the name Promise Keepers was an ideal choice because of the covenant God fulfilled through His Son. In Christ, God kept all the promises that He had made to mankind; and we as believers today rely upon God as the original Promise Keeper who enables us to keep our promises.

In 1993, after three years had been invested in laying a strong foundation, the original vision was realized as 50,000 men filled the stadium at the University of Colorado. From the impact of that one event, the idea began to grow increasingly larger, with more gatherings in more stadiums. Seven years later, in 2000, more than five million men had attended Promise Keepers conferences across America. Throughout those years of spectacular growth, and to this day, the original ideals have remained strong and firm. They are expressed in a

statement entitled "The Seven Promises of a
Promise Keeper:"

1. A Promise Keeper is committed to honoring
   Jesus Christ through worship, prayer and obe-
   dience to God's Word in the power of the
   Holy Spirit.

2. A Promise Keeper is committed to pursuing
   vital relationships with a few other men,
   understanding that he needs brothers to help
   him keep his promises.

3. A Promise Keeper is committed to practicing
   spiritual, moral, ethical, and sexual purity.

4. A Promise Keeper is committed to building
   strong marriages and families through love,
   protection and biblical values.

5. A Promise Keeper is committed to supporting
   the mission of his church by honoring and
   praying for his pastor, and by actively giving
   his time and resources.

6. A Promise Keeper is committed to reaching
   beyond any racial and denominational barriers
   to demonstrate the power of biblical unity.

7. A Promise Keeper is committed to influencing
   his world, being obedient to the Great
   Commandment (Mark 12:30-31) and the
   Great Commission (Matthew 28:19-20).

Whether you are male or female, these seven
ideals are valuable reminders in the stewardship of
your own commitments. Each one focuses on a

timeless principle to be taken to heart and put into practice. Several of these seven promises incorporate the all-important matter of spiritual accountability.

The American statesman Daniel Webster was once asked, "What is the greatest thought you have ever contemplated?" He replied, "The greatest thought I have ever had and the most important thing I have ever learned is that I am personally accountable to the God of all Creation." According to Romans 14:12, each one of us must give an account of ourselves directly to God. It is difficult to even imagine what that moment will be like; but I am certain that it will happen, and I want Him to say, "Well done, good and faithful servant."[11] I agree with Webster that there is no thought more sobering, but I would add that there is no motivation more powerful than the fact that we will face the Lord and give an account of our lives.

John Andrew Holmes quipped, "The entire population of the universe, with one little exception, is composed of *others*."

Accountability is also a governing principle in our relationships with other people. As John Andrew Holmes quipped, "The entire population of the universe, with one little exception, is composed of *others*." That "one little exception" is you. You do not exist in a vacuum, and your success will not be achieved in isolation. God has placed you in a world of people to whom you must relate and many of them are individuals to whom you are accountable. For example, God places spiritual leaders in positions of authority, and we are told in Scripture: "Obey your leaders and submit to their authority. They keep watch over you as men who must give an account. Obey them so that their work will be a joy, not a burden, for that would be of no advantage to you."[12] I find it so interesting in this verse that the accountability runs both ways: just as we are accountable *to* our spiritual leaders, they are accountable *for* us. As for the other relationships of life, the Bible says, "Let no debt remain outstanding, except the continuing debt to love one another, for he who loves his fellowman has fulfilled the law."[13]

The stewardship of commitment demands personal fidelity, integrity and devotion. It is a responsibility to fulfill with joy — a heartfelt decision to please the Lord in word, deed and attitude of heart.

Scripture References:

1 John 13:34-35
2 Philippians 1:3
3 See Philippians 1:4-8
4 See Philippians 1:5
5 Matthew 6:9-13
6 Matthew 7:7-8
7 Matthew 7:9-11
8 1 John 1:9
9 2 Corinthians 10:3-4
10 James 5:16
11 Matthew 25:21
12 Hebrews 13:17
13 Romans 13:8

CHAPTER 4

THE STEWARDSHIP OF TIME

CHAPTER 4

THE STEWARDSHIP OF TIME

Parkinson's.

A mere mention of the name brings images to the mind:

The still youthful face of Michael J. Fox, now twitching oddly in uncontrollable spasms.

The once potent hands of Muhammad Ali, now trembling and weak with the slightest effort.

For most people, these are the most prominent faces of Parkinson's, a disease that ravages the body with slow and unrelenting cruelty. But when I think of Parkinson's, I see another face: the gently smiling countenance of my own mother. I think back over the 31 years that she endured the endless torture of this sickness as it robbed her strength and stamina bit-by-bit, day-by-day until all the reserves were gone. As I write these words, just hours have passed since we laid Mom to rest near the small town in South Carolina where she entered this world 71 years ago. She had a long life; and even though her final three decades were punctuated with pain, she never complained. Each day to her was a gift, a treasure from God to be admired, appreciated and used to please Him. As I contemplate the stewardship of time, I think first of my Mom because it was at her knee that I learned to value and use time wisely.

God's Timely Invention

Philosophers over the ages have pondered the subject of time, ever striving to grasp its meaning. Many of them, of course, failed to recognize the most basic fact about time — that it was an invention of God. When He made this physical world, God created the sun and moon to distinguish day and night and, as Genesis explains, to "serve as signs to mark seasons and days and years."[1] Time is a relative marker for our lives but it has no constraints upon God because He is infinitely above it and beyond it. We need time markers, but God does not. In the eloquent prayer of Moses, the great prophet said, "For a thousand years in your sight are like a day that has just gone by, or like a watch in the night."[2]

The eminent theologian Francis Schaeffer often used the following diagram to illustrate as simply as possible the relevance of time to God.

The circle represents God in His eternal oneness. The line, suspended as it is within the circle, represents time. As sovereign over all, God's perspective on time is not limited in any way. He can view time at any moment of any era. As finite beings, we presently live within time; but He does not, and God is therefore not bound by the seasons and days and years of our earthly existence.

The "Eternal Now" of God

C. S. Lewis, one of the greatest Christian thinkers of the past century, offered this perspective on God's relationship to time: "To Him all the physical events and all the human acts are present in an eternal Now. The liberation of finite wills and the creation of the whole material history of the universe (related to the acts of those wills in all the necessary complexity) is to Him a single operation. In this sense God did not create the universe long ago but creates it at this minute—at every minute."

> Humans live in time and therefore attend chiefly to two things: to eternity itself and to the Present. For the Present is the point at which time touches eternity.
>
> — C. S. LEWIS

I will be very frank with you and admit that the writings of C. S. Lewis often make my brain ache! The depth of his ideas causes me to think long and hard, and I frequently will read one of his sentences or paragraphs several times. But I find that it's worth the effort because God gave him a remarkable understanding of biblical truths. In his famous book, *The Screwtape Letters*, in addressing this same subject, Lewis wrote, "Humans live in time and therefore attend chiefly to two things: to eternity itself and to the Present. For the Present is the point at which time touches eternity."

Rightly Numbering Our Days

We who are believers in Jesus Christ have received through Him the free gift of eternal life. Because we have eternal life, we do not see this life as the sum of our existence. From God's Word we take assurance in the fact that "our citizenship is in heaven"[3] and that life there is our ultimate destination. However, while we're here on earth, living in the dimension of time and space, it is imperative that we make the most of our days as each moment of our Present touches Eternity. The words of the ancient psalm are as relevant to us today as they were thousands of years ago: "Lord...Teach us to number our days aright, that we may gain a heart of wisdom."[4]

To rightly number our days is to allot our time wisely, to live in a way that pleases God and accomplishes His purposes. What does it mean, and how do we do it? Where do we look for a pattern to follow? The solution is not to buy a new Daytimer® or Franklin-Covey Planner® (though that may be a good idea). No, the first thing to do is to look to Jesus, to examine His life and determine how He spent His time. Obviously, this means you must look to the Scriptures, searching the pages of God's Word for timeless principles of time management.

Doing the Work of the Father

Have you ever examined how Jesus spent His days or analyzed His attitudes towards time? It is clear from the Gospels that in the stewardship of His time Jesus was never worried or hurried. There was never a sense of panic, never a moment of remorse for time lost. He was in all instances and in all circumstances doing the work of the Father, yet never displayed the classic symptoms of a workaholic, so driven by His purpose and absorbed by productivity that He forgot about people. In the years of His earthly ministry, Jesus spent time praying, teaching, helping, healing and interacting continually with men and women from all strata of society. But before that public ministry began, Jesus spent 30 years as a carpenter in the obscure village of Nazareth. We really have no idea how He spent his days there; but the implication of Scripture is that He was simply working like anyone else, His identity as Messiah virtually unknown. So, was He wasting time during those silent years? Of course not! In the cosmic calendar known only to God, those 30 years of quiet preparation enabled the three years of intensive, unprecedented service that we read about in the four Gospels.

> In the stewardship of His time, Jesus was never worried or hurried. There was never a sense of panic, never a moment of remorse for time lost. He was in all instances and in all circumstances doing the work of the Father, yet never displayed the classic symptoms of a workaholic...so absorbed by productivity that He forgot about people.

Jesus never became fixated on activity at the expense of the right attitude. In fact, His activity was always governed by His attitude. In writing to the Philippians, the apostle Paul expressed the essence of Jesus in this way:

Your attitude should be the same as that of Christ Jesus: Who, being in very nature God, did not consider equality with God something to be grasped, but made himself nothing, taking the very nature of a servant, being made in human likeness. And being found in appearance as a man, he humbled himself and became obedient to death—even death on a cross! Therefore God exalted him to the highest place and gave him the name that is above every name, that at the name of Jesus every knee should bow, in heaven and on earth and under the earth, and every tongue confess that Jesus Christ is Lord, to the glory of God the Father.[5]

Paul says that the attitude of Jesus should be our attitude as well. But how in the world is that possible? Fortunately, the answer is spelled out clearly in the verses immediately following Paul's lofty description of the attitude of Christ. And each point he makes is an essential element of the stewardship of time. Paul gives three specific and easy-to-remember instructions on this subject, so let's take a thorough look at each one.

• Work Out Your Salvation. (Philippians 2:12-13)

"Continue to work out your salvation with fear and trembling, for it is God who works in you to will and to act according to his good purpose."

First, to allay any misunderstandings, this statement does not mean to work *for* your salvation. It is not implying in any way that we can save ourselves. The idea that salvation can be earned is a very tempting notion, something that appeals to the human ego. We've all met people who say, "I never accept anything I haven't earned." But this is totally untrue, of course. Every one of us has been accepting unearned, undeserved blessings and benefits since the day we were born.

The verb that is translated "work out" in our English Bible is from a Greek term that means, "to work to full completion." It's the word we would use to communicate "working a field" or "working a math problem." But the true key to understanding this passage is the phrase which says, "For it is God who works in you." When you receive Christ, God begins to work in you. His working *in* you then enables you to work *for* Him. It's vital to understand that we're in this together, that we have a viable connection to Christ. That relationship is underscored by one biblical metaphor after another: we are clay, we are branches, we are vessels, we are ambassadors, we are soldiers, we are watchmen, we are servants. Notice that every one of these

> Our responsibility before God is underscored by one biblical metaphor after another: we are clay, we are branches, we are vessels, we are ambassadors, we are soldiers, we are watchmen, we are servants. Notice that every one of these implies responsibility — a responsibility to yield fully to Christ and to live in absolute obedience to Him.

implies responsibility — a responsibility to yield fully to Christ and to live in absolute obedience to Him.

• Shine Out Your Testimony. (Philippians 2:14-15)

"Do everything without complaining or arguing, so that you may become blameless and pure, children of God without fault in a crooked and depraved generation, in which you shine like stars in the universe."

If you ever have any doubt as to whether we live in a crooked and depraved generation, just a few minutes browsing through the headlines on CNN or Fox News will remove any uncertainties. And if you turn on the television to MTV you will be even more convinced. The values of this world have been twisted and distorted by the effects of sin, but the Christian measures life by the straight line of God's unfailing Word. Being "without fault" doesn't mean we are perfect but that we belong to Someone who is. And in this world, darkened as it is by impurities of all kinds, we are able to shine as bright lights. We are to be witnesses in this world, communicators who shine out a testimony of God's grace and hope in Jesus Christ.

• Hold Out the Word of Life. (Philippians 2:16)

"…as you hold out the word of life—in order that I may boast on the day of Christ that I did not run or labor for nothing."

God has spoken. He has given His Word. And His Word is of such power that it can create something out of nothing and give life to that which is dead. It is this transformational truth that we hold out to a completely secularized society that is estranged from God and ignorant of His principles. Only a Christian who is steeped in the Word can stand against the tide and hold out the Word of Life in a world like ours. But determination by itself is not enough; we must also have the energizing power of God's Spirit working in us. Jesus told His disciples, "As the Father has sent me, so send I you."[6] And so we go, in His name and with His authority.

Three Central Elements in the Stewardship of Time

Working out your salvation, shining out your testimony and holding out the Word of Life are three central elements in the stewardship of time. They are foundational to the wise, purposeful management of our days. Traditional approaches to time management deal with segmentation, prioritization, implementation and the like; but the bigger question when it comes to time management is not the degree of practical efficiency but the measure of spiritual effectiveness. If we are to be truly wise stewards we have to ask: What is really going to matter at the end of our earthly days? When we

Traditional approaches to time management deal with segmentation, prioritization, implementation and the like; but the bigger question when it comes to time management is not the degree of practical efficiency but the measure of spiritual effectiveness.

answer to God for our lives, what will be of greatest value?

Our highest priority is to be just like our Lord, giving ourselves wholeheartedly in service. None of us knows what tomorrow will bring, so there is no room for bold predictions. As James warned: "Now listen, you who say, 'Today or tomorrow we will go to this or that city, spend a year there, carry on business and make money.' Why, you do not even know what will happen tomorrow."[7] And then James says something even more sobering: "What is your life? You are a mist that appears for a little while and then vanishes. Instead, you ought to say, 'If it is the Lord's will, we will do this or that.' As it is, you boast and brag. All such boasting is evil. Anyone, then, who knows the good he ought to do and doesn't do it, sins."[8] While preaching on this passage of Scripture, Dr. Martin Luther King Jr. once said, "We must use our time creatively, forever realizing that the time is always right to do right."

> "We must use our time creatively, forever realizing that the time is always right to do right."
> — DR. MARTIN LUTHER KING JR.

The Measure of a Life

The measure of a life, from God's perspective, is not determined by its length but by its depth. In the final judgment (and there *will* be a final judgment), what will matter most is the depth of our devotion to God — how we stewarded our days in faithful service to Him, for Him and in His name.

The actual number of our years is irrelevant, a mere speck in the ocean of eternity. Whether we live to age 33 or to 103, our life span is, as James said, "a mist that appears for a little while and then vanishes." This doesn't mean that we cease to exist, but that our existence moves into an entirely new realm, a heavenly realm. But before we reach that point, before the moment comes for us to literally be with the Lord, we must live this life to the full. We must "redeem the time" — wisely investing the hours of each day.

Depth of devotion does not imply some kind of somber, monastic lifestyle. Devotion can be expressed at every level and in every activity of life. As Paul reminded the Corinthians, "Whether you eat or drink or whatever you do, do it all for the glory of God."[9] It is spiritually liberating and empowering to realize that everything — even the most mundane tasks — can be dedicated to God. Our hearts can be set on Him while our hands are set on the work we must do. In the Lord's eyes, there is no difference in value between the work of a surgeon and the work of a servant. It all comes down to a matter of motive: are we serving Him or serving ourselves? Are we seeking His glory or our gratification? The dichotomy between secular and sacred is a man-made division. To God, everything in our lives is sacred — sacred in the sense that it can be and must be devoted to Him.

> The dichotomy between secular and sacred is a man-made division. To God, everything in our lives is sacred — sacred in the sense that it can be and must be devoted to Him.

The Source of Satisfaction

The stewardship of time is a practical matter in that we have to make daily decisions about what to do. This is why we make lists and keep day-planners, and this can be a good thing so long as one does not become a prisoner of the planner. The best advice I can offer on the subject of time management is to choose a strategy, test it in the context of your own roles and responsibilities, and as long as it works, stay with it. If not, repeat the process until you find the system that adapts to you (rather than one to which you have to adapt). I have used all kinds of methods over the years, but I've learned that no matter what system I'm using I have to remind myself every day that I'm "spending" time: it is a commodity to be spent, just like money, and it must be valued as such. However, I must also remember the bottom-line truth: "This is the day that *the Lord* has made, I will rejoice and be glad in it."[10] The source of true happiness and satisfaction is not found in a program but in a Person, and it comes to the steward who lives to do the Master's will.

> I have used all kinds of methods over the years, but I have learned that no matter what system I'm using I have to remind myself every day that I'm "spending" time: it is a commodity to be spent, just like money, and it must be valued as such.

There is a fascinating story in the Gospel of Luke that occurred when Jesus was teaching in one of the synagogues.[11] His attention was drawn to a woman who was bent over and unable to stand straight. The Bible says that she "had been crippled by a spirit for eighteen years." Jesus called her forward and said to her, "Woman, you are set free from your infirmity."[12] Then He put His hands on her and she immediately straightened up and began to praise God. Seeing this happen, the ruler of the synagogue became indignant because Jesus had healed someone on the Sabbath day. He said to the people who were present: "There are six days for work. So come and be healed on those days, not on the Sabbath."[13] He was clearly unaware of the absurdity of his words until Jesus responded: "You hypocrites! Doesn't each of you on the Sabbath untie his ox or donkey from the stall and lead it out to give it water? Then should not this woman, a daughter of Abraham, whom Satan has kept bound for eighteen long years, be set free on the Sabbath day from what bound her?"[14] And the story concludes: "When he had said this, all of his opponents were humiliated, but the people were delighted with all the wonderful things he was doing."[15]

> In their minds, they were exercising the correct stewardship of time; however, in their system time had become more important than people.

The so-called religious leaders were concerned about compliance with a system — a system that had elevated the importance of a particular day to a level far beyond what God ever intended. In their minds, they were exercising the correct stewardship of time; however, in their system time had become more important than people, and adherence to the rules took precedence over profound human needs. Jesus' bold and compassionate act challenged both their ideas about time and their understanding of God's priorities. Jesus was telling them that if we truly love God we will truly love people, and we will do whatever it takes to steward our moments and days in a way that communicates that love. If we keep this in mind, and if we keep our eyes on Him, our stewardship of time will be truly purposeful.

Scripture References:

1   Genesis 1:14

2   Psalm 90:4

3   Philippians 3:20

4   Psalm 90:12

5   Philippians 2:5-11

6   John 20:21 (NKJV)

7   James 4:13-14a

8   James 4:14b-17

9   1 Corinthians 10:31

10   Psalm 118:24

11   See Luke 13:10-17

12   Luke 13:12

13   Luke 13:14

14   Luke 13:15-16

15   Luke 13:17

THE STEWARDSHIP OF OPPORTUNITY

CHAPTER 5

THE STEWARDSHIP OF OPPORTUNITY

I hate to miss an opportunity, and that day I missed a big one.

My best friend, David, called me and said, "Kirk, I want you go somewhere with me today."

"Where do you want to go?" I replied with a sense of hesitation, since I never know what he has up his sleeve.

"Germany," he said. And he stated it with the ease that one might have in saying, "I'm going to the mall."

"Germany!" I said. "Why in the world do you want me to go to Germany with you? And why do we have to do it today?"

"We have to go today," he answered, "because they're tearing down the Berlin Wall, and we have to see it. This is a once-in-a-lifetime opportunity. There's only one Berlin Wall, and once it's down, it's down."

I instantly knew that he was right, but I came up with so many excuses — meetings I had to attend, church services I had to plan, counseling sessions I had to conduct — and although I could have delegated, rescheduled or changed everything that was pending, I chose the path most traveled and I turned down the opportunity.

"Man, that would be a phenomenal thing to see," I told him, "but I just can't get away right now."

He tried a bit harder to convince me, but I still said 'no' — and I have regretted that decision for more than a decade and a half. Whenever I see images of those thousands of people in a frenzy of freedom bashing away at that despised wall with sledgehammers and picks and whatever else they could get their hands on, I wish that I had been there. I wish that I could have seen it firsthand. But I missed an opportunity because I chose to do the expected thing rather than the extraordinary.

> I wish that I could have seen it firsthand. I missed an opportunity because I chose to do the expected thing rather than the extraordinary.

Three years later, my friend called and once again said, "Kirk, I want you to go somewhere with me." And before he was able to tell me where we were going, I said, "When are we leaving?" I wasn't about to miss another chance to experience something of lasting significance. Startled by the quickness of my reply, he said, "It's a good thing you're so determined to go because where we're going is so unstable right now that we can't even get confirmed visas to enter the country. This is going to be an adventure." His cautions did not deter me. I was certain about this decision.

Our destination was Albania, a relatively small nation in southeastern Europe, bordered by Greece, Yugoslavia and Macedonia. Since 1944, Albania had been under communist rule, a staunch member of the Soviet bloc. For more than 40 years, Enver Hoxha ruled Albania with a ruthless disregard for human life. An avowed Stalinist, Hoxha confiscated farmland and commercial enterprises and established a totalitarian state. Untold thousands of people were killed for opposing his government, and thousands more were sent to internment camps and prisons. In 1967, Hoxha proclaimed Albania the world's first completely atheist nation. Following his death in the late 1980s, Albania was in complete disarray, a pathetic example of the folly of communism. A short time later, the USSR began to disintegrate and Christian missionaries began to enter the newly-freed eastern European nations. But Albania had become so isolated that no one knew what was happening there. We were about to find out.

> Albania had become so isolated that no one knew what was happening there. We were about to find out.

Walking into Albania's capital city, Tirana, was like stepping back in time. It looked like the faded image from a World War II history book. Nearly all the vehicles were from the 1940s and the city was drab and lifeless. I noticed that countless windows were covered with cloth, paper, cardboard — anything that would keep out the cold. Just before his death, Hoxha had ordered the army to break all the windows and destroy caches of food. The people looked shell-shocked, and they were clearly malnourished.

After getting a room at Tirana's only hotel, we began to explore the city. Along the way, we met a young lady who spoke English and she agreed to serve as our interpreter. Everywhere we went there was a buzz of conversation. The word was out that some Americans had come to town. Albanian military officers stopped us repeatedly and "fined" us for one infraction or another. We had pockets full of coins, so we would pay the equivalent of 10 or 15 cents and then be waved on. Every one of those young soldiers we met had an emptiness in his eyes. We left the center of town and began to wander down a side street. The scene that confronted us is one I will never forget.

> Every one of those young soldiers we met had an emptiness in his eyes. We left the center of town and began to wander down a side street. The scene that confronted us is one I will never forget.

A large number of people were crowded around some kind of compound. The stone wall surrounding the property could not be climbed over because jagged pieces of glass had been set into the top of the wall — a Third World version of barbed wire. But disregarding the danger, people were handing children over that wall! We made our way through

the crowd and reached the front gate of the compound. Seeing that we were foreigners, the military
police opened the gate and let us in. Once inside
those forbidding walls we looked around us and saw
a sea of children. We realized: This is why God sent
us here. This is an opportunity from Him.

We were ushered to the main building where
nurses greeted us with tears streaming down their
faces. They spoke to us excitedly
and urgently in their own language.
Following a small group of nurses,
we were shown one dimly-lit room
after another, and in each one we
saw children from wall to wall.
Hundreds of precious children
stared up at us, their dark eyes
seeming to plead with us for attention. The nurses were crying and
talking very rapidly, and our interpreter was doing her best to translate as quickly as possible. "We need
help...please help us...we have been
waiting for you to come...thank
God you are here...." We kept mov-
ing through the building, confront-
ed everywhere with the sight of children. On the
fourth floor, at the top of the stairs, lying on mats
strewn across the floor were scores of babies, each
wrapped papoose-style in rough burlap fabric. It was
difficult to keep our composure.

What in the world could we do here? We were
just two guys from South Florida, best friends since

> What in the world could we do here? We were just two guys from South Florida, best friends since our youth, both of us now pastoring churches. How could we respond to something so overwhelming?

our youth, both of us now pastoring churches. How could we respond to something so overwhelming?

The nurses took us to the basement, a damp, cave-like room that was nearly empty. The wood supply for the furnace was just about gone. The medicine cabinet was bare. The large refrigerator contained a block of cheese, some hard bread and one container of rancid milk. It was all they had left.

How could we make a difference? As teenagers we had once worked as volunteers in an orphanage; but this was almost too much to take in. We returned to our hotel to get our bearings, but soon the ring of an ancient phone sounded through the lobby. A few seconds later, my friend was asked to speak to someone on the phone. He stepped over to the desk to take the call, and after a very brief conversation returned to where I was standing. "Well," he said, "they're coming to pick us up. We're going to meet the new President of Albania."

Almost immediately we were picked up and taken with a full police escort to the presidential palace. Once inside we were greeted by President Sali Berisha and an entire entourage of officials. The president was curious as to why we had come and what we were doing in his country. While I was still mentally processing the question, my friend David answered, "We represent World Hope, and we're here to help the children." I looked at him and thought, *World Hope? What is World Hope? We're just two guys backed up by two churches and a few friends!*

The President was thrilled that Americans had finally come to his country, and he was appreciative that we wanted to help the suffering children. Within a couple of days he had given us the responsibility for the orphanage in Tirana and orphanages in four other cities. In our hotel lobby we put up a sign that read:

WORLD HOPE - Room #112

Changing the World One Child at a Time

Over the next two weeks we met with a constant stream of government officials and orphanage personnel. We were even successful in coordinating the emergency delivery of an entire planeload of food, medicine and relief supplies (paid for by U.S. Foreign Aid). There was, without exaggeration, one miracle after another as God made provision for an extraordinary situation. And there we were, just being His ambassadors in a place so desperately in need of His life-giving power. In the process, God gave birth to a ministry that is now touching lives on every continent. Its name, World Hope, was made up on the spur of the moment — but its impact has been long-lasting. We stewarded that opportunity and since then God has given us many, many more.

As I think back to that amazing time in Albania and reflect on what the stewardship of opportunity truly means, my heart is drawn to Ephesians 5:15-17. In the entire Bible, those verses for me are the most relevant on this subject. Take a moment and meditate on this admonition from the apostle Paul:

"Be very careful, then, how you live—not as unwise but as wise, making the most of every opportunity, because the days are evil. Therefore do not be foolish, but understand what the Lord's will is."

Let's explore the meaning of one phrase in particular: "making the most of every opportunity, because the days are evil." As we run life's race, we come across one opportunity after another; but we also encounter all sorts of obstacles along the way. The challenge is to gain the greatest value from the opportunities while avoiding or overcoming the obstacles. While he was in Ephesus, Paul sent a letter to the Corinthians describing an opportunity he had been given and the obstacles that came with it: "But I will stay on at Ephesus until Pentecost," he wrote, "because a great door for effective work has opened to me, and there are many who oppose me."[1]

> As we run life's race, we come across one opportunity after another; but we also encounter all sorts of obstacles along the way.

Paul was not intimidated by the fact that he had enemies bent on discrediting or even destroying him. He found confidence and great courage in the certainty that God had given him an opportunity for effective ministry, and he was determined to maximize that opportunity. That was the pattern of his entire life from the point of his conversion to the day he died as a martyr for Jesus Christ. Paul seized every chance he was given to declare God's truth, to demonstrate God's character and to encourage God's people. However, as he wrote on several occasions, he was able to make the most of his opportunities not because he was a great saint but because he was a humble servant. He never considered himself as one who had "arrived" at a state of total spiritual maturity. Instead, he kept pressing forward, redeeming the opportunities each step of the way. As he wrote to the Philippians, "I press on to take hold of that for which Christ Jesus took hold of me. Brothers, I do not consider myself yet to have taken hold of it. But one thing I do: Forgetting what is behind and straining toward what is ahead, I press on toward the goal to win the prize for which God has called me heavenward in Christ Jesus."[2]

As I read God's Word, I see other believers who, like Paul, show the importance of wisely stewarding one's God-given opportunities. I think of Joshua, who had spent 40 years in the wilderness as second-in-command to Moses, finally fulfilling the opportunity to lead the nation of Israel across the Jordan and into the land of promise. I think of Esther, who made the most of her opportunity to influence the king and save her people from certain genocide. I think of Nehemiah, who received news of a crisis, but saw it as an opportunity, and against all odds led the Jewish people of an entire city to rise up and build. We could study in depth any of these three remarkable individuals, but I direct your attention instead to another person who demonstrated the stewardship of opportunity in a truly memorable way. Her name was Deborah, which means "one who seeks." When we examine her life we indeed see someone who was always seeking God's will and seizing opportunities to bring Him glory.

Opportunity and the Power of Intuition

I have always been intrigued by the expression, "a woman's intuition." It isn't in the Bible, but I'm sure it's real. The evidence is undeniable that God blesses women with an intuitive ability that sometimes borders on the astonishing. A woman's intuition is often superior to a man's cold reasoning (or his pig-headedness, as the case may be). A lady once told me that if Pontius Pilate had taken the advice of his wife he would not have signed the death warrant for Jesus! She had a point, and I couldn't argue against it. I must admit that I have learned a great deal from the intuition of my mother, my wife, my daughter and a number of other significant women. In essence, they have taught me lessons in the stewardship of opportunity, because one of its major components is intuition.

> The evidence is undeniable that God blesses women with an intuitive ability that sometimes borders on the astonishing.

Deborah was blessed with a mighty portion of God-given intuition. She had flawless expertise as a leader, and God chose her to be one of the judges of Israel. She could read situations, read people and recognize opportunities. Judges 4:5 says, "She held court under the Palm of Deborah between Ramah and Bethel in the hill country of Ephraim, and the Israelites came to her to have their disputes settled."

In that era, palm trees were very rare in Palestine, so the tree itself was symbolic of Deborah's uncommon gifts and abilities. She matched intuition with inspiration as she poured out wisdom to everyone who sought her counsel.

Deborah's sphere of influence included everyone from peasants to kings. But with each person she stewarded the opportunity to give valued insight. From the shade of that palm tree, she confidently guided her nation, successfully resolving conflicts and rendering wise judgments. God blessed Deborah with prophetic knowledge of the military strategies Israel was to employ in battling their enemies.

> With each person she stewarded the opportunity to give valued insight. From the shade of that palm tree, she guided her nation, successfully resolving conflicts.

On one occasion she sent for Barak, an Israelite commander from Naphtali. She said to him: "The Lord, the God of Israel, commands you: 'Go, take with you ten thousand men of Naphtali and Zebulun and lead the way to Mount Tabor. I will lure Sisera, the commander of Jabin's army, with his chariots and his troops to the Kishon River and give him into your hands.'"[3]

Barak, although he was a brave man, was not as brave as Deborah. He said to her, "If you go with me I will go; but if you don't go with me, I won't go."[4] Rather than argue with him or try to convince him to change his mind, Deborah accepted Barak's reply and taught him an unforgettable lesson in the stewardship of opportunity. He would soon learn that an opportunity to exercise great power (such as he was given) is first an opportunity to exercise great faith. He should have known to take Deborah at her word and to seize the golden moment that he had been given. After all, she was speaking not her own word, but God's. Barak would still have a measure of success, but he would not experience the total success that would have been his through wholehearted faith.

"'Very well,' Deborah said, 'I will go with you. But because of the way you are going about this, the honor will not be yours, for the Lord will hand Sisera over to a woman.' So Deborah went with Barak to Kedesh, where he summoned Zebulun and Naphtali. Ten thousand men followed him, and Deborah also went with him."[5]

Opportunity and the Impact of Inspiration

For all we know, Barak may have thought that Deborah would be the woman to get the credit for total victory. But God had something else in mind. After the enemy forces had assembled in a massive front along the Kishon River, Deborah said to Barak, "Go! This is the day the Lord has given Sisera into your hands. Has not the Lord gone ahead of you?"[6] Like a fearless general, she shouted the command for engagement and the battle ensued. Inspired by Deborah's stirring words, Barak led the charge. "So Barak went down Mount Tabor, followed by ten thousand men."[7] Imagine what this must have looked like to the enemy. The passage goes on, "At Barak's advance, the Lord routed Sisera and all his chariots and army by the sword, and Sisera abandoned his chariot and fled on foot. But Barak pursued the chariots and army as far as Harosheth Haggoyim." And then the clincher: "All the troops of Sisera fell by the sword; not a man was left."[8]

Yes, it was a total rout; but it was not yet a total victory because Sisera had gotten away. For Barak, the supreme honor of the victory that day would have been to personally capture and slay Sisera. But it was not to be. "Sisera, however, fled on foot to the tent of Jael, the wife of Heber the Kenite, because there were friendly relations between Jabin king of Hazor and the clan of Heber the Kenite."[9] Sisera, the coward, had found what he thought to be a safe house. "Jael went out to meet Sisera and said to him, 'Come, my lord, come right in. Don't be afraid.' So he entered her tent, and she put a covering over him."[10] What a welcome sight for a soldier on the run: a gracious, hospitable woman willing to take him in. "I'm thirsty, he said, please give me some water." The story continues, "She opened a skin of milk, gave him a drink, and covered him up. 'Stand in the doorway of the tent,' he told her. 'If someone comes by and asks you, 'Is anyone here?' say 'No.'"[11] As Sisera gave these all-important instructions, the satisfying warmth of the milk was already starting to make him feel relaxed. He was

> It was a total rout, but it was not yet a total victory because Sisera had gotten away.

already completely worn out, and soon he was fast asleep on the floor of Jael's tent.

Opportunity and the Importance of Initiative

Jael was inspired by the opportunity that God had brought into her very tent, and she immediately took the initiative. The Bible says that "Jael, Heber's wife, picked up a tent peg and a hammer and went quietly to him while he lay fast asleep, exhausted. She drove the peg through his temple into the ground, and he died."[12] It was a gruesome scene, no doubt. But God had used a cagey woman to execute judgment on an enemy of His chosen people. We can only imagine the wily expression on her face when she broke the news to the Israelites. "Barak came by in pursuit of Sisera, and Jael went out to meet him. 'Come,' she said, 'I will show you the man you're looking for.' So he went in with her, and there lay Sisera with the tent peg through his temple—dead."[13] The passage concludes with these words: "On that day God subdued Jabin, the Canaanite king, before the Israelites. And the hand of the Israelites grew stronger and stronger against Jabin, the Canaanite king, until they destroyed him."[14]

> Jael was inspired by the opportunity that God had brought into her very tent, and she immediately took the initiative.

Jael saw the opportunity and did not hesitate; and God used her as a key figure in a great victory.

Some would condemn her act as cold-blooded murder, but the Song of Deborah in Judges 5 celebrates her initiative: "Most blessed of women be Jael, the wife of Heber the Kenite, most blessed of tent-dwelling women."[15] Barak, on the other hand, was actually rebuked by the fact that God had used Jael. His conditional obedience to the Lord brought conditional honor from the Lord. But Deborah received the highest blessing from God, because she had stewarded a great opportunity with great wisdom and absolute faith. In the final stanza of her song, Deborah says, "So may all your enemies perish, O Lord! But may they who love you be like the sun when it rises in its strength."[16] Then the chapter concludes with this powerful statement: "Then the land had peace forty years."[17] In a time of great calamity and chaos, peace came to Israel through the leadership of a godly woman who stewarded wisely and made the most of every opportunity.

> What are the opportunities that we are called upon to steward as believers of the 21st century?

Now, let's bring this down to where we live. What are the opportunities that we are called upon to steward as believers of the 21st century? As I look back at the opportunities God has already given me (and for which I must one day answer to Him), I see that the majority fall into three categories: Opportunities to Evangelize, Opportunities to Empathize and Opportunities to Energize. In each of these categories are priorities that I am convinced apply to every Christian.

Stewarding the Opportunity
to Evangelize

Think about the last words Jesus spoke to His disciples before He ascended back to heaven: "But you will receive power when the Holy Spirit comes on you; and you will be my witnesses in Jerusalem, and in all Judea and Samaria, and to the ends of the earth."[18] Just a few days before He made that dramatic, final statement, Jesus had said to them, "All authority in heaven and on earth has been given to me. Therefore go and make disciples of all nations, baptizing them in the name of Father and of the Son and of the Holy Spirit, and teaching them to obey everything I have commanded you. And surely I will be with you always, to the very end of the age."[19]

> Opportunities to spread the Gospel are to be used as if they were great riches. In fact, they are like great riches to the ones still waiting to hear, still waiting to know that Jesus is the only way, the only truth, the only life.

The "end of the age" as Jesus calls it is the end of the Church Age, the time from the coming of the Holy Spirit in power to the second coming of Christ in glory. That "age" is now 2,000 years long, and only God knows when it will end; but until it does, those who believe in Him have a crucial mission to fulfill. That mission — which is often called "The Great Commission" — is to evangelize the world and make disciples of Christ. "Evangel" means "Gospel," and evangelization is the spreading of the Gospel — the Good News of life and salvation through Jesus Christ. It is imperative to communicate this message because unless people put their faith in Christ, they are without hope.

Opportunities to spread the Gospel are to be used as if they were great riches. In fact, they are like great riches to the ones still waiting to hear, still waiting to know that Jesus is the only way, the only truth, the only life. Where and when do these opportunities come to us? They occur on the journey of life...

...in conversation with a friend who is going through a struggle...

...in meeting someone for the first (and perhaps only) time on a plane...

...in discussing eternal life with someone who is soon to leave this earthly life...

...in myriad opportunities that can come as brief snippets of time or in very lengthy and involved relationships.

Sharing the Gospel is an essential part of the Christian life. It is not a matter of personal preference, an "elective" in the school of discipleship. Nor is it a matter of personal performance, as if we by our own effort lead someone to Christ. The one who actually leads is the Holy Spirit, who draws souls to the Savior. But God has chosen to use us as His messengers in the process. We, the very ones who have found the Bread of Life, must tell everyone else about it. As we live from day to day, God gives us opportunities to sow the seed of His truth.

In the questions we answer, in the comments we make, in the opinions we share about a thousand-and-one different things, we can incorporate the truth of the Word and the message of the Gospel. But to seize the opportunities we must be ready. As Peter advised in his first epistle, "Always be prepared to give an answer to everyone who asks you to give the reason for the hope that you have."[20]

Stewarding the Opportunity to Empathize

> When we act with true Christian compassion we feel the emotional or spiritual pain of the other person, suffering with them just as Jesus did with all who came to Him for help or healing.

To empathize is to put yourself in another person's position — to identify with what they are thinking and feeling. We see this empathy in the beautiful example of the Good Samaritan, who looked upon the wounded man and had compassion on him.[21] The word *compassion* means, literally, "to suffer with another." When we act with true Christian compassion we feel the emotional or spiritual pain of the other person, suffering with them just as Jesus did with all who came to Him for help or healing.

The Samaritan was presented with what we would call a "can't-miss" opportunity to rescue a person in great distress. Two others had the same "can't-miss" opportunity before the Samaritan came along, and yet they missed it completely. Worse yet, they *chose* to miss it, willfully going to the other side of the road to escape the discomfort of getting too close to someone undesirable. They had exactly the same attitude we see today toward the homeless and profoundly poor of our own society. Many of us don't want to see them, much less get close to them and actually do something to lift them up physically, financially or spiritually.

The fact is, people all around us are in need of help and healing, just like the multitudes that Jesus looked upon with such pity that it made Him weep. But we're not just talking about feeling empathy for the down-and-outers; our compassion must extend to every human being with whom we relate, Christians and non-Christians alike. If we are going to be like Jesus, if we're going to seize the opportunities of life as He did, we must have His attitude — caring for those who are hurting, serving with humility, seeking always to please the Father.

> To *empathize* is to reactively feel what another person is feeling; to *energize* is to proactively affect how another person lives.

Stewarding the Opportunity to Energize

There is certainly a direct connection between empathizing and energizing, but there are some important distinctions. To *empathize* is to reactively feel what another person is feeling, but to *energize* is to proactively affect how another person lives. As believers indwelled by the Spirit of God, we have a resident energy source that He enables us to transmit. We have a God-given potential to do things that will strengthen those who are weak, not because of our power but by the energizing power of the Holy Spirit at work in us. We can say the right thing at the right time and give true encouragement, not to manipulate others but to motivate them to trust God.

We also have opportunities to energize when we stand for what is right. In an age that is increasingly anti-Christian in its demeanor, we will become more and more conscious of this challenge. But it is nothing new. The verses quoted at the beginning of this chapter bear a second look: "Be very careful, then, how you live—not as unwise but as wise, making the most of every opportunity, because the days are evil."[22] Notice especially the last phrase, "because the days are evil." These are, in fact, evil days — evil because this entire world system, so weighted down with sin and destruction, is against Christ, against the Bible and contrary to all that is good and right. A battle rages, and it will not end until Jesus comes. Until He does, we have opportunities to redeem. As we seize each one, let's remember some of the concluding words of Paul's letter to the Ephesians:

> *"Therefore put on the full armor of God, so that when the day of evil comes, you may be able to stand your ground, and after you have done everything, to stand. Stand firm then, with the belt of truth buckled around your waist, with the breastplate of righteousness in place, and with your feet fitted with the readiness that comes from the gospel of peace. In addition to all this, take up the shield of faith, with which you can extinguish all the flaming arrows of the evil one. Take the helmet of salvation and the sword of the Spirit, which is the*

word of God. And pray in the Spirit on all occasions with all kinds of prayers and requests. With this in mind, be alert and always keep on praying for all the saints.[23]

Scripture References:

1   1 Corinthians 16:8-9
2   Philippians 3:12-14
3   Judges 4:6-7
4   Judges 4:8
5   Judges 4:9-10
6   Judges 4:14
7   Judges 4:14
8   Judges 4:15-16
9   Judges 4:17
10 Judges 4:18
11 Judges 4:19-20
12 Judges 4:21
13 Judges 4:22
14 Judges 4:23
15 Judges 5:24
16 Judges 5:31a
17 Judges 5:31b
18 Acts 1:8
19 Matthew 28:18-20
20 1 Peter 3:15
21 See Luke 10:25-37
22 Ephesians 5:15-17
23 Ephesians 6:13-18

THE
STEWARDSHIP
OF
RESOURCES

CHAPTER 6

THE STEWARDSHIP OF RESOURCES

At 12:55 p.m. the mayday call crackled through the speakers at the Flight Service Station on Alaska's Kenai Peninsula. The desperate pilot of a Piper A22, a small single-engine plane, was reporting that he had run out of fuel and was preparing to ditch the aircraft in the waters of Cook Inlet. On board were four people, two adults and two young girls, ages 11 and 12. They had departed two hours earlier from Port Alsworth, a small community on the south shore of Lake Clark, bound for Soldotna, a distance of about 150 miles. Under normal conditions it would have been a routine flight; however, the combination of fierce headwinds and a failure to top off the fuel tank had created a lethal situation. Upon hearing the plane's tail number, the air traffic controller realized that his own daughter was one of the young passengers aboard the plane. In desperation himself, he did everything possible to assist the pilot; but suddenly the transmission was cut off. The plane had crashed into the icy waters.

Four helicopters operating nearby began searching the area within minutes of the emergency call; but they found no evidence of the plane, and no survivors. The aircraft had been traveling without water survival gear, leaving its four passengers with even less of a chance to make it through the ordeal. Fiercely cold Cook Inlet, with its unpredictable glacial currents, is considered among the most dangerous waters in the world. It can claim a life in minutes, and that day it claimed four.

For reasons we will never know, the pilot of that doomed aircraft chose not to use the resources that were at his disposal. He did not have enough fuel. He did not have the proper survival equipment. Perhaps he had not taken the time to get the day's weather report. Whatever the case, he did not use the resources that were available; and in this instance the consequences were fatal.

The stewardship of resources is a serious business; and God's will is that we give it serious attention. This demands that we have the right perspective on our resources, and that is possible only if we have the right focus on our *source*. Everything that we have — every earthly resource — comes from a heavenly source. God is our faithful supplier; and His plan is that we be His faithful stewards.

> The stewardship of resources is a serious business; and God's will is that we give it serious attention. This demands that we have the right perspective on our resources, and that is possible only if we have the right focus on our *source*.

THE STEWARDSHIP OF LIFE

Take an Inventory of Your Resources

The resources entrusted to us by God are to be stewarded wisely and purposefully. Our tangible resources fall into two basic categories: monetary and material. Monetary resources include your income and all the funds that you have in your bank accounts, savings accounts and redeemable investments. Material resources include all the things that have potential value in terms of Christian stewardship: your home, your vehicles and other earthly goods.

All resources, whether monetary or material, are the result of God's favor and blessing, not one's personal achievements. Therefore, the purpose in taking an inventory of these things is to quantify His blessings and consciously dedicate those resources to Him. In doing this we express to the Lord an attitude of stewardship versus one of ownership. "Our" resources actually belong to Him; but He gives us the privilege of using them, enjoying them and managing them for His glory.

> "Our" resources actually belong to Him; but He gives us the privilege of using them, enjoying them and managing them for His glory.

Follow the Investment Strategies that Lead to True Success

The God-given monetary and material resources in your life are to be invested in a way that brings the greatest return in spiritual terms. In the Lord's economy, things are different from any worldly system of financial management; and it is essential that we understand His principles and follow His plan.

How to use your money. Regardless of the amount of money you have, it can be stewarded in a wise and spiritually profitable manner. To put it as simply as possible, there are three things to do with your money:

1. Give it cheerfully to accomplish God-honoring purposes.

2. Spend it reasonably to meet personal needs and fulfill personal desires.

3. Save it strategically in order to extend value and to keep meeting needs in the future.

Concerning the first of these priorities — giving purposefully to the Lord's work — I could write an entire book. In fact, my colleague Dave Sutherland and I did write a book on this subject — *The 33 Laws of Stewardship* — which explores a whole range of biblical principles that govern how we live and how we give. This is a subject I deal with literally every day as I work with pastors and church leaders across America, helping them to realize their God-given vision for ministry. We deal with issues of strategic planning and coordination of major capital funding projects, usually to build or expand church facilities. When such a need arises it presents a different kind of challenge and requires a different kind of giving. The ongoing needs of a church's ministry are met through ordinary giving — ordinary in the sense of being regular and consistent. However, extraordinary needs must be met with extraordinary giving — above and beyond all normal commitments. My personal conviction is that the giving of the tithe isn't an option but a responsibility, and when I give it I am expressing confidence in the faith. Then, when I respond with an extraordinary gift to meet an extraordinary need of the church, I am expressing confidence in the future. In both kinds of giving, I have a sense of duty but also a great sense of delight, knowing that I am honoring the Lord and partnering with my fellow believers.

> The ongoing needs of a church's ministry are met through ordinary giving — ordinary in the sense of being regular and consistent. However, extraordinary needs must be met with extraordinary giving — above and beyond all normal commitments.

In financial terms, some of us have been blessed with a lot and some with very little, but we can all give generously, joyously and sacrificially. God's measurement is in proportion to what we have been given: to whom much is given, much is required, as Jesus said.[1] I have seen some very large financial gifts to the Lord's work (some well into eight figures), but I have learned that the smaller gifts can represent even more of a sacrifice. I know of a single mom with a couple of kids who gives in such a way that it affects deeply and costs greatly. Ultimately, the Lord decides and He rewards, but each one of us must be certain that we seek His purposes and His glory above everything else. In doing so, we are wise practitioners of the stewardship of resources.

How to use your things. If you love things and have an inordinate desire to have them, it can weigh you down and impede your spiritual progress. But the proper attitude toward the things of this world can have a liberating effect. Three keys that I have learned are these:

1. Enjoy things, but don't cherish them. God is not opposed to our enjoying His blessings upon us. As J. B. Phillips says, He isn't leaning over the balcony of heaven just waiting for us to enjoy something so that He can say, "Cut that out!" No, the Lord is pleased when His children find pleasure in what He has given. However, our attachment must be to Him, not to the things themselves. "Set your affections on things above, not on earthly things," says Colossians 3:2.

> This is how sharing should be — giving of our things joyfully, not because we feel obligated or duty-bound. God loves a cheerful giver, not a reluctant one.

2. Share things joyfully, not reluctantly. It's good to share from our material possessions because in sharing we can bless others just as God has blessed us. Some dear friends of mine were once faced with a great financial need as they prepared to return to the mission field. Their plan had been to sell their car and all their household goods prior to their departure, but they felt strongly impressed by the Lord to give away everything instead. With great joy they handed over the keys to their car to a needy couple, and to a local church they gave all their belongings to furnish a house for visiting missionaries. As an expression of love, that same church took up a surprise offering for my friends and presented them with a check that amounted to more than double what they could have received from selling their car and furnishings. God blessed them, they blessed others, and then God blessed them again! This is how sharing should be — giving of our things joyfully, not because we feel obligated or duty-bound. God loves a cheerful giver, not a reluctant one.

3. Think like a pilgrim, not a settler. The lyrics of an old gospel song say, "This world is not my home, I'm just a passin' thru. My treasures are laid up, somewhere beyond the blue." It sounds very corny, but it's actually true and it is based upon the words of Jesus Himself: "Do not store up for yourselves treasures on earth, where moth and rust destroy, and where thieves break in and steal. But store up for yourselves treasures in heaven, where moth and rust do not destroy, and where thieves do not break in and steal. For where your treasure is, there your heart will be also."[2] We are indeed pilgrims, not settlers. As Paul reminded the Philippians, "our citizenship is in heaven."[3]

Remember the Insights that Make a Lasting Difference

In the stewardship of resources it is vital to think biblically. I encourage you to take to heart these important insights:

1. Remember to use things and love people (not vice versa). Things have a way of capturing our interest and arresting our affections. It is amazing, in fact, how much of a pull money and material things can have upon us, making us elevate their importance completely out of reason. God's design is that we use things and love people, but what often happens is that we use people and love things! John wrote, "Do not love the world [that is, this temporal world in which we live] or the things in the world. For if anyone loves the world, the love of the Father is not in Him."[4]

Once while He was teaching the multitudes, Jesus was interrupted by a man who blurted out, "Teacher, tell my brother to divide the inheritance with me."[5] Jesus responded with words that exposed the man's true problem of greed: "Watch out! Be on your guard against all kinds of greed; a man's life does not consist in the abundance of his possessions."[6] What a powerful summation of what matters. It's not about things; it's about people. It's not about us; it's about God.

> God's design is that we use things and love people, but what often happens is that we use people and love things!

2. Remember that little things can make a big difference. I vividly recall a sermon preached by my pastor when I was just a teenager. He began his message by holding up a smooth stone, like one you would find in a streambed. "Little things can make a very big difference," he said, as he began a brilliant exposition of the story of David and Goliath.[7] The giant Goliath, the mightiest warrior of the Philistine forces, towered to a height of "six cubits and a span." By today's measurements he stood nine feet nine inches tall — more than two feet taller than the tallest man in the NBA! Every morning and evening for 40 days he had blustered and threatened the army of Israel, led by King Saul. "Send out your best man to fight me," Goliath shouted. "If I win, you will be our slaves. If he wins, we will be your slaves." But there were no takers, and the level of fear in the Israelite camp was increasing. Then David showed up, sized up the situation and offered to face the giant foe. Refusing the king's armor, David went to face Goliath armed with only a leather sling and five stones. Of course, David prevailed by slinging one of those smooth stones with absolute precision. It sailed through the air and thudded rudely into Goliath's forehead. A little thing had made a big difference.

> In the stewardship of resources it is so true that "little is much if God is in it." He can take the smallest gift, like the widow's mite, and multiply its effectiveness far beyond what we could ever imagine.

In the stewardship of resources it is so true that "little is much if God is in it." He can take the smallest gift, like the widow's mite, and multiply its effectiveness far beyond what we could ever imagine. Whatever the size of the resource, it can be used to honor God and accomplish His purposes.

3. Remember that you can gain everything, but still be a big loser. It was one of the most sobering questions Jesus ever asked: "What shall it profit a man if he gain the whole world and lose his own soul?"[8] This world is full of people who have amassed great wealth and put full confidence in their riches. But every one of them will in an instant abandon all that they have accumulated; and unless they have "laid up treasure in heaven" as Jesus admonished, they will die as losers of the worst sort. Whatever you "gain" in this world has true value only to the extent that it is invested and stewarded with an eye toward eternity.

4. Remember that you can give all you have, yet invest it all as well. One of the wondrous paradoxes of the Christian life is that whatever you give away in Jesus' name produces not a loss but a profit — a spiritual profit that accrues in a heavenly account. The God-honoring steward is not one who holds on to wealth but who is willing to let go of it and give it away for that which is most important. The famous explorer and missionary David Livingstone had this attitude toward worldly resources. In his journal he wrote, "I place no value on anything I have or may possess, except in relation to the kingdom of God. If anything will advance the interests of the kingdom, it shall be given away or kept, only as by giving or keeping it I shall most promote the glory of Him to whom I owe all my hopes in time or eternity."

> Whatever you give away in Jesus' name produces not a loss but a profit — a spiritual profit that accrues in a heavenly account.

5. Remember that you will give an account to God. Accountability is a subject we looked at earlier, but it's helpful to mention it once again. I try to remind myself every day to live in a way that will prepare me to stand before the Lord and give a good account of my stewardship. I want to be faithful and wise in managing all that God has entrusted to me, not because I think it will determine my eternal salvation but because it is a gift that I can give to Him who gave me life itself.

6. Remember to be willing to give and willing to give up. I love the biographies of missionary pioneers because there is a raw beauty in their devotion to Christ and their determination to extend the frontiers of the Gospel. Many of their stories are filled with examples of the exceptional stewardship of resources. In his book, *The Living Faith*, Lloyd Douglas recounts an episode in the life of missionary Thomas Hearne: "In his journey to the mouth of the Coppermine River, Hearne wrote that a few days after they had started on their expedition, a party of Indians stole most of their supplies.

> I want to be faithful and wise in managing all that God has entrusted to me, not because I think it will determine my eternal salvation but because it is a gift that I can give to Him.

His comment on the apparent misfortune was: 'The weight of our baggage being so much lightened, our next day's journey was more swift and pleasant.' Hearne was en route to something very interesting and important; and the loss of a few sides of bacon and a couple of bags of flour meant nothing more than an easing of the load. Had he been holed in somewhere, in a cabin, resolved to spend his last days eking out an existence, and living on capital previously collected, the loss of some of his stores by plunder would probably have worried him almost to death."

How we respond to "losing" some of our resources for the sake of the Lord's work depends upon whether we are on the move or waiting for our last stand.

7. Remember that the way to multiply your trust is by trusting the Multiplier. Each one of us is given a trust and we are charged with the responsibility of multiplying that trust for the Lord. This is fundamentally a matter of faith: we multiply our trust by trusting the Multiplier. God wants us to rely upon Him, to seek His favor, to pray for His blessing. Faith is foundational to effective stewardship.

Since the summer of 1992 I have made an annual hunting and fishing trip to Alaska. My mentor and partner on these mini-expeditions has been my dear friend, Dr. Jerry Prevo. Jerry is the senior pastor of Alaska's leading church, and he has had huge influence in shaping the state's cultural and political landscape. He is also an accomplished bush pilot and outdoorsman. Jerry is one of those friends whom you can count on in a crisis, who always takes your side, and who is a man's man! As a hunter he has few equals, with seven world-class Dall sheep trophies alone. We have shared some unforgettable times of fellowship in some of the most spectacular settings imaginable in America's fabled "last frontier." We have also faced some moments of great danger and high adventure. Every landing on the tundra or mountains is a nail-biter! But the most memorable of all our trips was the first one.

I hadn't even gone to Alaska to hunt. I was there to tour the Alaska National Wildlife Project and to be the guest speaker at my friend's church. Just to visit Alaska was the fulfillment of a lifetime dream and this was my first trip! Jerry had invited me to stay a few days longer and go hunting with him. I eagerly accepted and we flew into a remote region of the Alaska Range, about 150 miles west of Anchorage near the Mulchatna Valley. We landed on a mountain top for glassing with our binoculars, set up our tent, tied down the plane and began looking for animals. On our first night we spotted some caribou and focused in on one particular bull. The next morning we put a stalk on him, got close and I decided to harvest him. It was awesome! After boning out the meat and salvaging the cape and horns, we loaded the plane, tied the horns on the wing and flew right off the mountain top.

We passed a mountainside where a number of black bears and a few grizzlies were feeding on berries. My license allowed me to hunt a black bear and we made a split-second decision to go for it.

On our way back we passed a mountainside where a number of black bears and a few grizzlies were feeding on berries. I had never seen anything like it. My license allowed me to hunt a black bear and we made a split-second decision to go for it. Jerry looked for a place to land and then brought the plane down into the tundra, bouncing to a rest. We deplaned, unloaded the gear and set up the tent. Then Jerry took off for Anchorage to drop off the caribou meat and pick up additional supplies. As the plane droned off into the distance I surveyed my resources: a tent, my sleeping bag, a gallon jug of water, a lantern, some waterproof matches, a box of granola bars, a hunting knife, a rifle and five bullets.

The plan was for Jerry to return that night, but when the skies began to darken about 1 a.m. and he had not come back, I was beginning to consider that something bad had happened. Although I was so tired, I couldn't sleep. Every time the tent shook I thought one of those grizzlies was coming in.

The plan was for Jerry to return that night, but when the skies finally began to darken about 1 a.m. and he had not come back, I was beginning to consider that something very bad had happened. Although I was so tired, I couldn't sleep. Every time the sides of the tent shook in the wind I thought one of those grizzlies was coming in. I laid there holding my borrowed rifle. Earlier that day Jerry and I had flown through Merrill Pass and he had shown me the relics of downed planes from years past and also some very recent ones. I couldn't help but think that my friend had crashed like so many others in the wilds of Alaska. I fought against letting my mind go there. Yet, Jerry had described the effect of rapid weather changes, planes running out of fuel because of powerful headwinds, pilot error and all sorts of other disconcerting things. Now I suspected that he, too, had fallen victim. How would I get word to someone, to anyone for that matter? How would anyone know that I had not been on that plane with him?

I didn't sleep at all the first night. Somehow on the second night I began to doze off, but awakened every few minutes at the howling of the wind. When the morning dawned I realized that I was all alone in a vast, remote area. That was before the days when GPS devices and satellite phones were commonplace, and I was literally out of touch with civilization of any kind. My only means of communication was a small signal mirror in a small emergency kit. The stark reality of my situation began to set in. I thought about my precious wife, Denise, and my kids back in Miami, holding them in my heart but frustrated with the impossible distance between us. I thought: *If I have to, I will walk through the mountains to get back to them.* I promised Denise that I would come home. Then I thought about my friend and his dear family, hoping against hope that he was still alive. As the hours passed with excruciating slowness I became more and more determined to survive, to somehow make it through this ordeal with God's help. More than ever in my life I needed to practice the stewardship of resources.

> When the morning dawned I realized that I was all alone in a vast, remote area. That was before the days when GPS devices and satellite phones were commonplace.

On the first day, expecting Jerry to return quickly, I had eaten the entire box of granola bars. What a mistake! I began to think: *I'm using too much of the lantern fuel for light. I need to conserve everything, especially food and water.* Everything I had learned as a Cub Scout and Sea Scout, especially all those articles I had read in *Outdoor Life* magazine and all of the stories I had heard over the years began to come back. I knew that my main challenges would be not to panic, to conserve my bullets, to find food and water and to stay dry. On a brief hike away from the tent I made my first stalk on a black bear and shot it. I cleaned the meat as best I could and started frying it in the lantern top. That was my best idea. For five desperately long days, one day at a time, I stayed focused on survival. I read my Bible, prayed, kept my wits about me, watched for bears (especially grizzlies) and thought about my family. In my mind, no one knew where I was, nor could anyone have known that I was not aboard the plane with Jerry. He was such a good pilot that it was hard to imagine that he had gone down, but it was Jerry himself who told me the weather in Alaska is so unpredictable and potentially violent.

I made the decision to walk out on the sixth day if Jerry hadn't come back or someone else hadn't

> For five desperately long days, one day at a time, I stayed focused on survival. I read my Bible, prayed, kept my wits about me, watched for bears (especially grizzlies) and thought about my family. In my mind, no one knew where I was.

spotted me. I wrote a note to leave at the campsite in case someone happened upon it; and when I had finished writing that very difficult message, I loaded my pack and started down the mountain. All at once I heard the most beautiful sound — the distant sound of a plane engine. I tried to spot it above the trees. At first it was just a speck. I ripped open my pack and got out the binoculars. I looked again and saw a plane with unmistakable orange and tan markings — Jerry's plane!

The sight of that high-winged, humble bush plane with its big tundra tires was the sweetest thing I had ever seen! Jerry circled and made his approach. As soon as the wheels hit the ground I began to run toward the plane. When Jerry climbed out of the plane I could see that he was all right and I was so happy that he was OK. He greeted me with a big hug (and he's not a hugging type of guy), and said, "I'm so glad you're alive! I'm so glad you're OK!" I was shocked to hear those words and, of course, I wanted to know why he hadn't come back right away. He said, "I couldn't fly!" I had no idea what he was talking about. "Why?" I asked. He explained, "The volcano erupted and the weather went down, so no one was allowed to fly. In fact, I had to fly just above the river and tree tops to get here!" When I asked, "What volcano?" Jerry was stunned. "You mean you didn't know that Mt. Spurr erupted right after I left you here?" I assured him that I had no idea about any volcanic eruption. "But there was a massive earthquake at the time the mountain blew," Jerry said.

We were less than 12 miles away from the volcano but I hadn't felt a thing, and we figured out that it was because I was on tundra that had absorbed the shock like a thick, heavy carpet.

Soon we had all the gear packed and stowed and we were on our way back to Anchorage. Along they way, he was pretty quiet and so was I, each of us filling in the details for the other between silent pauses. I had learned a lot about the stewardship of resources during those five incredibly intense days. The constant challenge to wisely use everything that was available (and to find the things that weren't) had reminded me what really matters in life. A short time later I was on the long flight home to Miami, not in a pine box but in a coach seat that seemed remarkably comfortable. On that 5,000-mile jour-ney I counted and recounted God's blessings. He had graciously protected my friend and provided for me in the midst of an astonishing experience. I was so grateful to the Lord for enabling me to steward what I had and to appreciate everything, literally everything. My faith had increased, but beyond that I cherished my wife more, I loved my family more and I cared for my church more deeply than ever. As my faith was increasing during those days it occurred to me that my most significant resource is prayer. My long conversations with the Lord while stranded in that wilderness reminded me that the place may be desolate, but He will never leave me in desolation. I have been back to that same region of Alaska many times in the years since that pivotal week in 1992, and each time I go there I realize anew that the challenges of life can seem so over-whelming at times, but we have to put it all in proper perspective — an eternal perspective. The stewardship of resources is a temporal responsibility, but its impact and its importance are eternal.

Scripture References:

1   See Luke 12:48b (KJV)

2   Matthew 6:19-21

3   Philippians 3:20

4   1 John 2:15 (NKJV)

5   Luke 12:13

6   Luke 12:15

7   See 1 Samuel 17:1-54

8   Luke 9:25 (KJV)

THE STEWARDSHIP OF YOU

CHAPTER 7

THE STEWARDSHIP OF YOU

Sometimes I read the Bible and catch myself laughing out loud. Almost always, I'm chuckling because I see myself in the frailties and failures of people described in various stories of the Scriptures. It happened just the other day when I was reading the familiar account of God's call to Moses. I think we Americans often imagine Moses as actually looking and acting like Charlton Heston in *The Ten Commandments*. But, of course, he was probably nothing at all like that. And his reactions to the call of God are hardly that of a hero. The Lord had appeared to Moses very dramatically, drawing his attention to a bush that burned but was not consumed by the flames. God then spoke to Moses and told him of the bold mission on which he was to embark. His response was to immediately begin asking questions and making excuses. *Who am I to do this? What would I say? Who would believe me?* And to each doubting question, God would give the reassurance of His enabling power. Finally, Moses asks one question too many and God gives him an object lesson. Let's read the incident as it is described in the first verses of Exodus, chapter 4...

> *Moses answered, "What if they do not believe me or listen to me and say, 'The LORD did not appear to you'?"*
>
> *Then the LORD said to him, "What is that in your hand?"*
>
> *"A staff," he replied.*
>
> *The LORD said, "Throw it on the ground."*
>
> *Moses threw it on the ground and it became a snake, and he ran from it.*
>
> *Then the LORD said to him, "Reach out your hand and take it by the tail."*
>
> *So Moses reached out and took hold of the snake and it turned back into a staff in his hand.*
>
> *"This," said the LORD, "is so that they may believe that the LORD, the God of their fathers— the God of Abraham, the God of Isaac and the God of Jacob—has appeared to you."* [1]

The Defining Question

Notice the question that God asks Moses: "What is that in your hand?" No other question could be more relevant to our own lives, because God wants to take whatever we have and turn it into an instrument of His power. He wants to perform a miracle of transformation in order to use us in His service in an extraordinary way. Like Moses, we may have become too accustomed to the day-in, day-out regularity of life; and God sometimes decides to upset our routines. In Moses' case, his life had already been divided into two eras: as a prince in Egypt from birth to age 40, and as a shepherd in the desert from age 40 to 80. Moses had fled from Egypt, running for his life after a misguided, murderous attempt to identify with his people. In the remote loneliness of the desert he had brooded over that failure for four long decades. He was undoubtedly gripped with a feeling of hopelessness about the Hebrew nation — who were not really a nation so much as an unorganized mob of slaves in Egypt. Then, it happened: God suddenly intervened and called Moses to the high adventure of service.

As we know, Moses did not react with excitement and eagerness to meet the challenge. To the contrary, he was dismayed and instantly overcome with doubts about himself and about how the Hebrew people would react to his intervention. Understandably, he felt inadequate for the mission and unfit for the task. He tried to get out of it, but God replied with amazing assurances that He would be with him, that the people would believe him, and even that the Egyptians would be favorably disposed toward Moses and the Israelites. Yet, after all of the

Notice the question that God asks Moses: "What is that in your hand?" No other question could be more relevant to our own lives, because God wants to take whatever we have and turn it into an instrument of His power.

Lord's promises, Moses was still reluctant to commit. At that point, God asked, "What is that your hand?"

Significance in the Insignificant

The staff that Moses held in his hand was the tool of his trade as a shepherd. It represented who he was — an ordinary man with ordinary equipment. When Moses threw down the staff it became a snake; and when he picked it up it again became a wooden rod. There was nothing in the staff, nor in the life experience it stood for, to equip Moses in any way for the job of leading an entire nation out of bondage. And yet God wanted to use that shepherd's staff to make a vital point: God's will is to use the weak things to confound the mighty, to transform an object of little value into an awesome weapon that can break down the walls of opposition. It seems so insignificant, yet God wanted Moses to surrender his staff, to give it up and see what it really was — a symbol of the sinister, snake-like tendencies within his own heart and the complete inadequacy of his own abilities and resources.

> God's will is to use the weak things to confound the mighty, to transform an object of little value into an awesome weapon that can break down the walls of opposition.

When the staff became a snake, Moses ran from it. I doubt that any of us have ever seen an 80-year-old man move so quickly! But God called him back, and told Moses to pick up the slithering, dangerous snake by the tail. By faith (and I'm sure it took a lot of faith), he did what God told him to do; and the snake instantly became a rod in his hand once again. But this time, something was different. The staff, symbolic of Moses' life, had been surrendered for God's use and had become an instrument of spiritual authority. From that day forward, Moses increasingly realized that the simple wooden stick in his hand was representative of an infinite power — a power that would capture the attention of millions of people. Having grown up in Pharaoh's palace, Moses was not naive about the confrontation that lay ahead. He knew that the Egyptian king would be resistant and that the Israelite slaves would be frightened by the prospect of a revolt against their oppressors. But Moses knew that he was in the hand of God, as surely as the rod was in his own hand.

As we read further in the book of Exodus we discover that the staff is thereafter referred to as "the rod of God." It no longer belongs to Moses, for it has been surrendered to the Lord and is endued with His strength. It is the rod in Moses' hand when God brings judgment upon Egypt in the ten plagues. It is the rod lifted high as God splits the waters of the Red Sea. It is the rod which strikes the rock at Horeb, bringing streams of water from a boulder. In every instance, the "rod of God" is used to demonstrate His power and provision. And, tragically, it was the self-willed use of the rod which resulted in the greatest disappointment of Moses' life — a solemn reminder to us against using for selfish purposes anything that has been consecrated to God.

Who God Chooses and Who He Uses

There is an innate tendency to think that only those persons who have remarkable skills and brilliant minds are the truly useful in God's service.

The first question regarding the stewardship of your life is the same question that God asked Moses: "What is that in your hand?" There is an innate tendency to think that only those persons who have remarkable skills and brilliant minds are the truly useful in God's service. But this question rebukes that idea. It's wrong to think that you could serve God more effectively if only you were more articulate, more intelligent or more gifted than someone else. The fact is that God loves you and wants you just as you are; yet He sees in you not what you are, but what you can be in His hand. Jesus called as His disciples a rag-tag bunch of fishermen, a wild-eyed zealot, a despised tax collector and a few other less-than-desirable members of society. But that motley crew was used by Him to "turn the world upside down,"[2] according to the book of Acts. No person is more useful in the Lord's service than any other person who is equally obedient and yielded to God. The true measure of value is not one's prominence, superiority or popularity, but one's faith in God and commitment to Him. What we may view humanly as limitations or disabilities count for nothing in God's economy. This is a highly personal matter: God is asking what is in *your* hand.

Joni Eareckson was a vivacious teenager on a family vacation when she dove into shallow waters and struck her head on a rock. In one horrific instant she was left a quadriplegic for life, permanently disabled from the neck down. Through years of physical therapy and seemingly endless medical procedures, Joni endured a personal tribulation that few of us can fathom. According to her autobiography there were times that she despaired over not being able to take her own life, frustrated that her unresponsive limbs kept her from ending it all. But into the darkness of Joni's despair, God turned on the floodlight of His grace. Through the witness of loving friends — who saw her as a person, not a victim — Joni came to faith in Jesus Christ. Putting her trust fully in the Lord, she yielded her life for Christian service. In spite of all her physical liabilities and limitations, Joni was ready and willing to be used by God.

> What we may view humanly as limitations or disabilities count for nothing in God's economy. This is a highly personal matter: God is asking what is in *your* hand.

More than 30 years have passed since Joni Eareckson Tada committed her life to Christ, and to say that she has been remarkably used by God since that day is quite an understatement. She is a best-selling author, an acclaimed artist and an internationally renowned speaker. Her life story was the subject of a widely distributed motion picture. Her works of art — done entirely by mouth with a paintbrush clinched in her teeth — have inspired countless people the world over. But Joni's greatest influence is through the organization that bears her name, Joni & Friends, which ministers to handicapped persons in dozens of countries, providing support programs, resources and thousands of wheelchairs. This "disabled" woman has turned out to be one of most able and effective persons of our generation, a shining example of a life fully devoted to Christ.

> This "disabled" woman has turned out to be one of most able and effective persons of our generation, a shining example of a life fully devoted to Christ.

Answering God's Question

When we consider God's question to us — "What is that in your hand?" — we must realize that He isn't necessarily referring to something literal. Unlike Moses, we don't always carry around the tools of our trade or our identity. However, what we do have in common with Moses is this: In the same way that God called upon Moses to give everything he had, He calls upon you and me to do the same. He wants us to willingly offer ourselves in His service and for His purpose. Joni Eareckson understood this; and though she literally could not hold a staff in her hand, her yielded life has become a "rod of God" raised in spiritual triumph. The fact is that what any one of us actually has to offer to God is inconsequential. We are finite and He is infinite. But through His miraculous empowerment we are able to do His will on earth.

So, again we face the question: What is that in *your* hand?

I have entitled this chapter "The Stewardship of You," realizing that I take the risk that some people will misconstrue the meaning. It is not my intention to encourage a self-centered mindset (which much of today's motivational literature does). To the contrary, I urge you to think about yourself without thinking selfishly. In other words, always remember who you are and why you are here. You are a human being, created by a loving God, designed in His image and destined for His purposes. You are special in His eyes, and you have a role to play in His eternal plan. In fulfilling that unique role, wise stewardship is imperative. Every blessing and benefit in your life is a factor in the stewardship equation. Your spiritual gifts, your natural abilities, your acquired skills, your material resources, your personal desires — all these and more are categories on the balance sheet of your life. How you manage these God-given resources determines your success as a steward.

> Always remember who you are and why you are here. You are a human being, created by a loving God, designed in His image and destined for His purposes.

As we head down the home stretch of this book, there are two final topics of lasting relevance: Your Spiritual Gifts and Your Spiritual Calling. Let me comment briefly on each one.

The Stewardship of Your Gifts

A spiritual gift is a Spirit-endowed ability for Christian service. It is purely an expression of grace, as indicated by the very word used in Scripture: our English word *gift* is from the Greek term *charisma*, which is derived from *charis*, the Greek word for *grace*.

As a loving Father, God gives spiritual gifts to every one of His children. Simply stated, a spiritual gift is a Spirit-endowed ability for Christian service. It is purely an expression of grace, as indicated by the very word used in Scripture: our English word *gift* is from the Greek term *charisma*, which is derived from *charis*, the Greek word for *grace*. Two distinct passages of the New Testament, Romans 12:6-8 and 1 Corinthians 12:8-10, describe spiritual gifts and explain their purpose. When Christians are taught to identify their spiritual gifts and encouraged to exercise those gifts within a body of believers, then the church will function normally.

A spiritual gift is not a talent. Non-Christians have talents as well as Christians, but only Christians are spiritually gifted. Talents derive from natural ability, but spiritual gifts are the result of spiritual endowment. Talents instruct, inspire or entertain on a natural level; but gifts are for building up other believers or reaching out to unbelievers. Something supernatural occurs when a spiritual gift is exercised. Nothing supernatural occurs when a talent is used. Talents and gifts do have a relationship, but they are not one and the same.

There are several elements in the process of learning and using your spiritual gifts:

Awareness. Study God's Word and know what it says on this important subject.

Belief. Trust in the truth that God has given you spiritual gifts to be used in His service. By grace, He gives the gifts; by faith, you put them into practice.

Confirmation. Prayerfully seek God's direction, asking Him to confirm the identity and reality of your spiritual gifts. Be aware that He will often use other Christians to reinforce your sense of confirmation.

Distinction. Don't confuse natural talents with spiritual gifts, but recognize that one can be employed in the exercise of the other.

Exercise. Put your gift into practice. Exercise it at every opportunity that God brings your way.

Throughout this process, ask meaningful questions: What do I seem equipped to do? What opportunity is at hand that I'm in a position to respond to? What are my deepest spiritual desires? How do I fit in with the other members of this body of believers? What are the needs that I am most moved to meet? Do others (especially spiritual leaders) recognize my gift(s) and appreciate my involvement? The answers to these questions can shed a lot of light and give a better understanding of your function within the Body of Christ.

The Stewardship of Your Calling

Romans 11:29 states this monumental truth: "For God's gifts and his call are irrevocable." When God endows you with His gifts and extends His call to your life, He doesn't later change His mind and retract what He has given. As James says, "Every good and perfect gift is from above, coming down from the Father of the heavenly lights, who does not change like shifting shadows."[3] The first and foremost of His gifts is, of course, the gift of the new birth, granting us eternal life through His Son. "He chose to give us birth through the word of truth, that we might be a kind of firstfruits of all he created."[4] Our first calling, then, is a calling to salvation — to believe and receive Jesus Christ as Savior and Lord. By His Holy Spirit, God calls us to Himself and gives us His life. When we respond in faith, He then calls us to a life of Christ-centered service.

> When God endows you with His gifts and extends His call to your life, He doesn't later change His mind and retract what He has given.

Since the Bible is filled with stories of God's call to service, it is very difficult to single out a particular example. We could examine God's call to Abraham, directing him to leave his homeland and journey by faith to an unnamed land. We could explore the fascinating experience of Gideon, who struggled against doubts to follow God's directives. We could study the extraordinary story of Esther, who was called by God to literally save her people from annihilation. We could delve deep into the life of Paul, called to service as he lay blinded in the dust of a Damascan road. Any of these individuals could teach us so much about the stewardship of one's calling, but the person from whom I have learned the most on this subject is the apostle Peter. Perhaps it's because I can identify so readily with his bull-in-the-china-shop impulsiveness or his highly emotive relationship to Jesus. Whatever it is, his life speaks to me and he has taught me some priceless lessons in stewardship.

Peter was one of the first two men called by Jesus to be His disciples. He and his brother, Andrew, left their fishing nets and followed the man they knew to be the Messiah. Peter was an eyewitness of the Lord's ministry, and with James and John was a member of the "inner circle" of the Twelve. After the resurrection of Christ and His ascension to heaven, Peter and the other disciples waited and prayed until the Spirit came upon them. On the day of Pentecost, the promised power came, and they began to declare the Good News. Peter was the central character in the drama that unfolded, preaching the first sermon of a new era. Acts 2 describes that amazing experience, and the chapters that follow give insight into the key factors in following the call of God.

Spiritual Confidence. The Bible tells us that one day after Pentecost when Peter and John were going up to the temple at the time of prayer, they were confronted by a beggar who had been crippled since birth. He asked them for money, but they gave him something far better: "Then Peter said, 'Silver or gold I do not have, but what I have I give you. In the name of Jesus Christ of Nazareth, walk.' Taking him by the right hand, he helped him up, and instantly the man's feet and ankles became strong. He jumped to his feet and began to walk."[5] A crowd quickly gathered to see this miraculous thing, and Peter seized the opportunity to preach the Gospel. For their outrageous "crimes," the religious authorities threw Peter and John in jail for the night.

On the next day, when Peter and John were called before the ruling council, Peter once again began to preach. The Bible says that he was filled with the Spirit as he boldly declared the name and power of Christ and unashamedly proclaimed Jesus as the only way. He said to them, "Salvation is found in no one else, for there is no other name under heaven given to men by which we must be saved."[6] His words were startling to religious rulers who were not used to such blatant preaching. They were dumbstruck by the boldness of Peter and John.

> Peter and his fellow disciple John were uneducated, untrained men. There wasn't anything exceptional about them, yet they caused the highest-ranking religious leaders to marvel at them.

Peter and his fellow disciple John were uneducated, untrained men. They were simple fishermen, coarse and unsophisticated. I wouldn't be surprised if people of that day told "fisherman" jokes! There wasn't anything exceptional about them, yet they caused the highest-ranking religious leaders to marvel at them. Just a few weeks before, however, Peter had denied that he even knew Jesus. What happened to cause such an astonishing change? Actually, several things: Jesus had died, He had risen from the dead, He had ascended back to heaven's glory, and the Holy Spirit had come as promised in fullness of power. Peter, along with the other disciples, was an eyewitness and a participant in these history-making events. He had been changed — indeed, he was still being changed — conformed to the character of Christ by the power of the Holy Spirit. As for the council, Acts 4:13 says, "When they saw the courage of Peter and John and realized that they were unschooled, ordinary men, they were astonished and they took note that these men had been with Jesus." As you steward God's calling in your life, an essential element is spiritual confidence. Natural, human logic (and nearly all self-help books) say to believe in yourself, to follow your instincts, to confide in your abilities and intelligence. But I can tell you that true satisfaction and success come through believing in God and confiding in the Spirit's power — just like Peter learned to do.

He had been changed — indeed, he was still being changed — conformed to the character of Christ.

Spiritual Conformity. Spiritual confidence must always be coupled with spiritual conformity — that is, conformity to Christ. As you steward God's calling in your life, ask yourself on a consistent basis: Am I becoming more like Christ? Is my life reflecting His character? You see, the evidence of a changed life is incontrovertible and it often leaves the skeptics speechless. That's what happened in this incident with Peter and John: "But since they could see the man who had been healed standing there with them, there was nothing they could say."[7] There they sat, that august body of religious leaders. Their faces were stern, their eyes firing daggers of hate at Peter and John. But their tongues were frozen. They could say nothing against what had happened. A man paralyzed for life had been healed. A good deed had been done. Yet they refused to acknowledge the overwhelming evidence of God's working. They admitted that a miracle had been done, but refused to admit that God had done it. They were "religious" but unbelieving, diametrically opposed to Christ and His followers — just like it is today in nations around the world.

The council warned Peter and John not to speak or teach in the name of Jesus. Blinded by pride and arrogance, they simply didn't want to hear any more of this. But the disciples were ready to give an answer: "Judge for yourselves whether it is right in God's sight to obey you rather than God."[8] The matter was so clear and convincing that all the authorities could have honestly said was, "Obey God rather than us." But they didn't. Instead, they threatened and blustered. Their hope was to maintain control by the threat of force, but it was simply not going to work. Peter and John chose to follow Christ, to conform to His will and to confide in the Spirit's power. "For we cannot help speaking about what we have seen and heard,"[9] they replied.

Spiritual Conviction. The third element in the stewardship of God's calling is an unbending spiritual conviction about who God is, who you are and what your reason for being is. You acknowledge that God is your loving Father who saves you through His Son and empowers you by His Spirit. You realize that you are, as Paul said, "chosen…according to the plan of him who works out everything in conformity with the purpose of his will."[10] And you agree that the purpose of your life is to honor your Lord by communicating His truth, demonstrating His character and seeking His pleasure. Your all-encompassing reason to get up every morning is to seize the day for God's glory.

> Making the most of all that you have and all that you are doesn't come down to you. It comes down to *"Christ in you*, the hope of glory."

Making the most of all that you have and all that you are doesn't come down to you. It comes down to *"Christ in you*, the hope of glory."[11] Thankfully, the stewardship of life is not an endless list of chores but an ever-increasing abundance of God's blessing on the one who seeks Him earnestly, loves Him wholeheartedly and follows Him unreservedly.

On Thursday, July 8, 2004, at 6:45 in the morning, my mom passed from this life into eternity with
her Lord. For nearly all of her adult life she had
lived for the Lord, for my dad and for her family.
For the last 31 of those years she struggled against
the constant downward pull of Parkinson's disease,
never once complaining or being concerned for her
own needs. Those final few days with her are vivid
in my mind. Mom and Dad had been married for
50 years and three months, and as I watched my
dad sit by her side during those waning hours, I
could see more than ever how they were truly one.
They never had much in the ways that the world
measures worth, but they were actually quite rich in
more important ways.

It had been my privilege to have them live with
us the last nine years. On their 50th wedding
anniversary we surprised them with a great number
family and friends, and one of my dad's best friends
said to me, "I will never forget when your dad and
I traveled home from the Korean War for the wedding. When I looked at your mom I knew she loved
him completely." How right he was. The years they
were together, and especially the last hours they
shared, made me realize what Mom loved about
Dad. She loved his character, his faithfulness to her,
his work ethic, his love for his boys, his commitment to church on Sundays, his dependability in
always bringing his paycheck home to her. Those
qualities in the end are all that matter anyway.
In her last talk with me the Sunday before her
"homegoing," she said, "Kirk, I have loved you for

all of your life...you take care of my family for me now."

My wife, Denise, was holding my mom's hand on that bright Thursday morning, singing "It is Well with My Soul" when Mom stepped into the presence of God. Denise said, "I loved your mother like she was my own. That God chose me to be sitting with her holding her hand when He called her home was my greatest honor in life. Peggy was the most like Jesus of any person I have ever known." It was my wife's birthday and she said, "This is God's present to me."

Just like my mom had done for so long, Denise was there, sitting in the chair of responsibility, stewarding a precious opportunity and gaining a priceless gift.

For me, that moment said so much about the stewardship of life. It's about love, devotion, diligence and all the other things we have touched upon in this book. But, above all, it's about faithfulness.

So then, men ought to regard us as servants of Christ and as those entrusted with the secret things of God. Now it is required that those who have been given a trust must prove faithful.[12]

May the God of all faithfulness give you strength and wisdom to be a faithful steward in His name.

Scripture References:

1   Exodus 4:1-5

2   Acts 17:6 (KJV)

3   James 1:17

4   James 1:18

5   Acts 3:6-8

6   Acts 4:12

7   Acts 4:14

8   Acts 4:19

9   Acts 4:20

10   Ephesians 1:11

11   Colossians 1:27

12   1 Corinthians 4:1-2